Corporate Tax Statistics 2024

OECD

BETTER POLICIES FOR BETTER LIVES

This work is published under the responsibility of the Secretary-General of the OECD. The opinions expressed and arguments employed herein do not necessarily reflect the official views of the Member countries of the OECD.

This document, as well as any data and map included herein, are without prejudice to the status of or sovereignty over any territory, to the delimitation of international frontiers and boundaries and to the name of any territory, city or area.

The statistical data for Israel are supplied by and under the responsibility of the relevant Israeli authorities. The use of such data by the OECD is without prejudice to the status of the Golan Heights, East Jerusalem and Israeli settlements in the West Bank under the terms of international law.

Note by the Republic of Türkiye
The information in this document with reference to "Cyprus" relates to the southern part of the Island. There is no single authority representing both Turkish and Greek Cypriot people on the Island. Türkiye recognises the Turkish Republic of Northern Cyprus (TRNC). Until a lasting and equitable solution is found within the context of the United Nations, Türkiye shall preserve its position concerning the "Cyprus issue".

Note by all the European Union Member States of the OECD and the European Union
The Republic of Cyprus is recognised by all members of the United Nations with the exception of Türkiye. The information in this document relates to the area under the effective control of the Government of the Republic of Cyprus.

Please cite this publication as:
OECD (2024), *Corporate Tax Statistics 2024*, OECD Publishing, Paris, https://doi.org/10.1787/9c27d6e8-en.

ISBN 978-92-64-50081-5 (print)
ISBN 978-92-64-50955-9 (PDF)
ISBN 978-92-64-56493-0 (HTML)

Corporate Tax Statistics
ISSN 2958-485X (print)
ISSN 2958-4434 (online)

Revised version, January 2025
Details of revisions available at: https://www.oecd.org/about/publishing/corrigenda.htm

Photo credits: Couverture © Shutterstock.com.

Corrigenda to OECD publications may be found at: https://www.oecd.org/en/publications/support/corrigenda.html.

Foreword

This is the sixth edition of *Corporate Tax Statistics*, an annual publication that brings together information on corporate taxation and base erosion and profit shifting (BEPS) practices that previously were unavailable to tax policy researchers and policymakers. This includes data on corporate tax rates, revenues, effective tax rates (ETR), tax incentives for research and development (R&D) and innovation, and withholding taxes amongst other data series. *Corporate Tax Statistics* also includes anonymised and aggregated Country-by-Country Reporting (CbCR) data providing an overview on the global tax and economic activities of thousands of large multinational enterprise groups operating worldwide. *Corporate Tax Statistics* follows on from the OECD/G20 BEPS Project and its package of fifteen measures adopted in 2015 to address tax avoidance. The project's Action 11 noted that the lack of available and high-quality data on corporate taxation is a major limitation to the measurement and monitoring of the scale of BEPS and the impact of the measures agreed to be implemented under the OECD/G20 BEPS Project.

The report is structured as follows. Chapter 1 presents internationally comparable data on the tax revenues of OECD, Latin American and the Caribbean (LAC), African, and Asian and Pacific jurisdictions. Chapter 2 contains information on the headline tax rate faced by corporations and can be used to compare the standard tax rate on corporations across jurisdictions and over time. Chapter 3 presents information on standard and treaty-based withholding taxes (WHTs) which are levied on businesses when they make payments to other foreign or domestic business entities or individuals, e.g., in the form of dividends, interest, and royalties. Chapter 4 presents "forward-looking" ETRs, which are synthetic tax policy indicators calculated using information about specific tax policy rules to assess the impact of taxation on returns to a hypothetical investment project. Chapter 5 describes several indicators of R&D tax incentives that offer a complementary view to the standard ETRs in Chapter 4 with a focus on tax support provided through expenditure- and income-based R&D tax incentives.

Chapter 6 contains information on several BEPS actions, notably Action 3 relating to Controlled Foreign Company rules, Action 4 relating to interest limitation rules, Action 5 relating to intellectual property regimes and Action 13, relating to CbCR. As part of BEPS Action 13, CbCR was introduced to support jurisdictions in combating BEPS. An overview of the anonymised and aggregated CbCR data is provided in Chapter 7, including general data characteristics, limitations, and some general observations from the CbCR data.

This publication was prepared under the auspices of the Working Party No. 2 on Tax Policy and Statistics of the Inclusive Framework (IF) on BEPS. The authors wish to thank delegates of Working Party No 2 for their time in preparing the statistics for publication. The publication is led by Ruairi Sugrue, under the supervision of Pierce O'Reilly. Chapters 1, 2 and 3 were prepared by Ruairi Sugrue. Chapter 4 was prepared by Clara Gascon, Ana Cinta Gonzalez Cabral and Felix Hugger. Chapter 5 was prepared by Ana Cinta Gonzalez Cabral, with input from Silvia Appelt and Fernando Galindo-Rueda. Chapter 6 was prepared by Ruairi Sugrue with input from Jessica De Vries and the Forum for Harmful Tax Practices (FHTP). Chapter 7 was prepared by Ruairi Sugrue and Felix Hugger.

Table of contents

FIGURES

TABLES

Reader's guide

Overview

In developing this 2024 edition of the *Corporate Tax Statistics* database, the OECD has worked closely with members of the Inclusive Framework (IF) on base erosion and profit shifting (BEPS) and other jurisdictions willing to participate in the collection and compilation of statistics relevant to corporate taxation.

This database is intended to assist in the study of corporate tax policy and expand the quality and range of data available for the analysis of base erosion and profit shifting. The *Measuring and Monitoring BEPS, Action 11 - 2015 Final Report* highlighted that the lack of quality data on corporate taxation is a major limitation to the measurement and monitoring of the scale of BEPS and the impact of the OECD/G20 BEPS project. While this database is of interest to policy makers from the perspective of BEPS, its scope is much broader. Apart from BEPS, corporate tax systems are important more generally in terms of the revenue that they raise and the incentives for investment and innovation that they create. The *Corporate Tax Statistics* database brings together a range of information to support the analysis of corporate taxation, in general, and of BEPS, in particular.

The database compiles new data items as well as statistics in various existing data sets held by the OECD. The sixth edition of the database contains the following categories of data:

- Corporate tax revenues;
- Statutory corporate income tax (CIT) rates;
- Standard withholding tax rates and bilateral tax treaties;
- Corporate effective tax rates;
- Tax incentives for research and development (R&D);
- Action 13 implementation;
- Controlled foreign company (CFC) rules;
- Interest limitation rules;
- Intellectual property (IP) regimes;
- Anonymised and aggregated Country-by-Country Reporting statistics.

Box 1. *Corporate tax statistics* database

Corporate tax revenues:

- data are from the OECD's Global Revenue Statistics Database;[1]
- covers 123 jurisdictions from 1965-2021 (for OECD members) and 1990-2021 (for non-OECD members);

Statutory CIT rates:

- covers all IF jurisdictions[2] from 2000-2024;

Standard withholding tax rates:

- data covering all IF jurisdictions from 2022 – 2024;

Bilateral tax treaties:

- data covering 144 jurisdictions (including all IF jurisdictions);

Corporate effective tax rates:

- covers 90 jurisdictions for 2017-2023;

Tax incentives for R&D:

- four indicators produced by the OECD Centre for Tax Policy and Administration and the OECD Directorate for Science, Technology and Innovation;
  - covers 48 jurisdictions for 2019-2023 (for preferential tax treatment for R&D, based on effective average tax rates and cost of capital for R&D, including income-based and expenditure-based tax incentives);
- data are from the OECD R&D Tax Incentive Database[2] produced by the OECD Directorate for Science, Technology and Innovation;
  - covers 48 jurisdictions for 2000-2023 (for expenditure-based tax and direct government support as a percentage of R&D);
  - covers 48 jurisdictions for 2000-2023 (for implied subsidy rates for R&D, based on the B-Index);

BEPS actions:

- **Action 3:** Data controlled foreign company rules;
- **Action 4:** Data on interest limitation rules;
- **Action 5:** IP regimes - data collected for 2018-2024 by the OECD's Forum on Harmful Tax Practices, which covers 61 regimes in 46 jurisdictions for 2024;
- **Action 13:** information on the implementation of the minimum standard on Country-by-Country Reporting

Anonymised and aggregated CbCR statistics:

- data are from anonymised and aggregated CbCR statistics prepared by OECD Inclusive Framework members and submitted to the OECD;
- covers up to 52 headquarter jurisdictions and up to 217 affiliate jurisdictions for 2016-2021.

Notes:

1. https://www.oecd.org/tax/tax-policy/global-revenue-statistics-database.htm.
2. Covers 143 IF members as of the 1st January 2024.
3. https://www.oecd.org/innovation/tax-incentives-RD-innovation/.

Abbreviations and acronyms

ACE	Allowance For Corporate Equity
BEPS	Base Erosion and Profit Shifting
BERD	Business Expenditure On R&D
CbCR	Country-By-Country Reporting
CFC	Controlled Foreign Company
CIT	Corporate Income Tax
ETR	Effective Tax Rate
EATR	Effective Average Tax Rate
EMTR	Effective Marginal Tax Rate
FDI	Foreign Direct Investment
FHTP	Forum On Harmful Tax Practices
GDP	Gross Domestic Product
GTARD	Government Tax Relief for Business R&D
ICAP	International Compliance Assurance Programme
IF	Inclusive Framework On BEPS
IP	Intellectual Property
ILR	Interest Limitation Rule
LAC	Latin American and The Caribbean
MNE	Multinational Enterprise
NPV	Net Present Value
R&D	Research And Development
RPR	Related Party Revenues
SMEs	Small And Medium-Sized Enterprises
STR	Statutory Tax Rate
TREAT	CbCR Tax Risk Evaluation and Assessment Tool
UPE	Ultimate Parent Entity
UPR	Unrelated Party Revenues
WHTs	Withholding Taxes

Names and ISO codes of jurisdictions covered

ISO Code	Name	Iso Code	Name	ISO Code	Name
ALB	Albania	GAB	Gabon	NZL	New Zealand
AND	Andorra	GEO	Georgia	NIC	Nicaragua
AGO	Angola	DEU	Germany	NER	Niger
AIA	Anguilla	GHA	Ghana	NGA	Nigeria
ATG	Antigua And Barbuda	GIB	Gibraltar	MKD	North Macedonia
ARG	Argentina	GRC	Greece	NOR	Norway
ARM	Armenia	GRL	Greenland	OMN	Oman
ABW	Aruba	GRD	Grenada	PAK	Pakistan
AUS	Australia	GTM	Guatemala	PAN	Panama
AUT	Austria	GGY	Guernsey	PNG	Papua New Guinea
AZE	Azerbaijan	GUY	Guyana	PRY	Paraguay
BHS	Bahamas	HTI	Haiti	PER	Peru
BHR	Bahrain	HND	Honduras	PHL	Philippines
BGD	Bangladesh	HKG	Hong Kong (China)	BOL	Plurinational State of Bolivia
BRB	Barbados	HUN	Hungary	POL	Poland
BEL	Belgium	ISL	Iceland	PRT	Portugal
BLZ	Belize	IND	India	QAT	Qatar
BEN	Benin	IDN	Indonesia	COG	Republic of the Congo
BMU	Bermuda	IRL	Ireland	ROU	Romania
BTN	Bhutan	IMN	Isle Of Man	RWA	Rwanda
BIH	Bosnia And Herzegovina	ISR	Israel	KNA	Saint Kitts And Nevis
BWA	Botswana	ITA	Italy	LCA	Saint Lucia
BRA	Brazil	JAM	Jamaica	VCT	Saint Vincent and the Grenadines
VGB	British Virgin Islands	JPN	Japan	WSM	Samoa
BRN	Brunei Darussalam	JEY	Jersey	SMR	San Marino
BGR	Bulgaria	JOR	Jordan	SAU	Saudi Arabia
BFA	Burkina Faso	KAZ	Kazakhstan	SEN	Senegal
CPV	Cabo Verde	KEN	Kenya	SRB	Serbia
KHM	Cambodia	SWZ	Eswatini, Kingdom of	SYC	Seychelles
CMR	Cameroon	KOR	Korea	SLE	Sierra Leone
CAN	Canada	KGZ	Kyrgyzstan	SGP	Singapore
CYM	Cayman Islands	LAO	Lao People's Democratic Republic	SVK	Slovak Republic
TCD	Chad	LVA	Latvia	SVN	Slovenia
CHL	Chile	LSO	Lesotho	SLB	Solomon Islands
CHN	China	LBR	Liberia	ZAF	South Africa
COL	Colombia	LIE	Liechtenstein	ESP	Spain
COK	Cook Islands	LTU	Lithuania	LKA	Sri Lanka
CRI	Costa Rica	LUX	Luxembourg	SWE	Sweden
CIV	Côte D'Ivoire	MAC	Macau, China	CHE	Switzerland
HRV	Croatia	MDG	Madagascar	THA	Thailand
CUB	Cuba	MWI	Malawi	TGO	Togo
CUW	Curaçao	MYS	Malaysia	TKL	Tokelau
CZE	Czechia	MDV	Maldives	TTO	Trinidad And Tobago

ISO Code	Name	Iso Code	Name	ISO Code	Name
COD	Democratic Republic of The Congo	MLI	Mali	TUN	Tunisia
DNK	Denmark	MLT	Malta	TUR	Türkiye
DJI	Djibouti	MRT	Mauritania	TCA	Turks And Caicos Islands
DMA	Dominica	MUS	Mauritius	UGA	Uganda
DOM	Dominican Republic	MEX	Mexico	UKR	Ukraine
EGY	Egypt	MCO	Monaco	ARE	United Arab Emirates
SLV	El Salvador	MNG	Mongolia	GBR	United Kingdom
GNQ	Equatorial Guinea	MNE	Montenegro	USA	United States
EST	Estonia	MSR	Montserrat	URY	Uruguay
FRO	Faroe Islands	MAR	Morocco	UZB	Uzbekistan
FJI	Fiji	NAM	Namibia	VUT	Vanuatu
FIN	Finland	NRU	Nauru	VNM	Viet Nam
FRA	France	NLD	Netherlands	ZMB	Zambia

Executive summary

***Corporate Tax Statistics* is an annual publication intended to assist in the study of corporate tax policy and expand the quality and range of data available for the analysis of base erosion and profit shifting (BEPS).** This includes data on corporate tax rates, revenues, effective tax rates, and tax incentives for research and development (R&D) and innovation, withholding tax rates and tax treaties, Intellectual Property (IP) regimes, and BEPS Actions. *Corporate Tax Statistics* also includes anonymised and aggregated Country-by-Country Reporting (CbCR) data providing an overview on the global tax and economic activities of thousands of multinational enterprise groups operating worldwide.

This year's publication includes several expansions to the available data. The 2024 edition contains new data on the effective tax rates available to MNEs on highly mobile intangible assets through IP regimes and other similar measures. The publication also includes new data on the variation of MNEs effective tax rates within jurisdictions. Updates to information on BEPS Actions 3 and 4 on Interest Limitation Rules (ILR) and Controlled Foreign Company (CFC) rules, as well as an expansion in the coverage of the data on withholding tax rates are also included. The main findings of the report are as follows:

- **Corporate tax revenues continue to make an important contribution to jurisdictions' economies, with modest increases relative to the previous year.** In 2021, the share of corporate tax revenues in total tax revenues was 16.0% on average across the 123 jurisdictions for which corporate tax revenues are available in the database, and the share of these revenues as a percentage of Gross Domestic Product (GDP) was 3.2% on average.
- **The data point to a continued stabilisation of corporate tax rates.** Statutory corporate income tax rates (STRs) remain stable in the period between 2021 and 2024, arresting their long-term decline over the last two decades, though rates remain far below historic averages. The average combined (central and sub-central government) STR for all Inclusive Framework jurisdictions covered declined dramatically from 28.0% in 2000 to 21.7% in 2019. From 2019 to 2024, the average STR has remained relatively stable with a rate of 21.7% in 2019 and 21.1% in 2024.
- **Effective Average Tax Rates (EATRs) have continued to decline modestly.** Looking at the development of the composite EATRs from 2017 and 2023, the unweighted average composite EATR has declined steadily over this period, from 21.6% in 2017 to 20.2% in 2023. This decline has slowed since 2019 and EATRs have remained relatively stable on average, with modest declines in median EATRs. Average EATRs were 20.9% in 2019 and 20.2% in 2023, while median EATRs were 22.8% in 2019 and 22.7% in 2023.
- **Some signs of stabilisation of corporate tax rates could also be seen in a stabilization of the tax subsidies being provided for R&D investments.** While R&D incentives can provide important tax support for R&D and innovation, they are also often seen as a means of attracting mobile intangible investment which can be subject to strong competitive pressures. Tax subsidies for R&D have stabilised and have even reduced slightly in recent years, with the average subsidy reducing EATRs for R&D by 34.8% in 2020, 35.3% in 2021, 34.7% in 2022 and 33.4% in 2023.

- **The data continues to point to the existence of base erosion and profit shifting, though there are some signs of modest reductions in recent years.** High-level indicators of potential BEPS activity have fallen in investment hubs relative to their values four years prior. These indicators include median revenues per employee (which has fallen by 13.1% relative to its 2017 value), median profits per employee (which has fallen by 16.1%), and median related party revenues as a share of total revenue (which has fallen by 11.5%). While these indicators could reflect reduced BEPS behaviour, the report noted that the 2021 CbCR data could also be affected by the COVID-19 crisis. Moreover, all these indicators remain far higher in investment hubs relative to other jurisdictions, pointing to the continued existence of BEPS activity.
- **Most IP regimes covered in the database have been found to be not harmful by the OECD Forum on Harmful Tax Practices.** Under the Action 5 BEPS peer review process, the OECD Forum on Harmful Tax Practices identified 61 IP regimes in place across 46 jurisdictions in 2024. Forty-three regimes in total were found to be not harmful; 26 of these regimes were found to be not harmful after having been amended to align with the Action 5 minimum standard.
- **The 2024 edition of *Corporate Tax Statistics* continues to expand the data available to study MNE activity.** It includes anonymised and aggregated CbCR data on the activities of over 8 000 multinational enterprises (MNEs) worldwide, including new data on the variation of MNEs' effective tax rates within jurisdictions. These new data show the presence of low-taxed profit in high-tax jurisdictions, which are likely the result of tax incentives and other targeted concessions. These low-taxed profits highlight the revenue-raising potential of the global minimum tax, even in jurisdictions that would be considered high-tax based on an analysis of average tax rates alone.
- **In addition, this year's edition increases and expands several other data series.** The coverage of statistics on Withholding Tax rates (WHT) has expanded significantly. This dataset consists of tax rates on dividends, interest and royalty payments that are applicable as of the 2024 fiscal year. This year's publication also contains updates to previously published datasets on Interest Limitation Rules (ILR) and Controlled Foreign Company (CFC) rules continuing the expansion of *Corporate Tax Statistics* to provide additional data to tax researchers and policymakers alike.

1 Corporate tax revenues

Key insights

- In 2021, the share of corporate tax revenues in total tax revenues was 16.0% on average across the 123 jurisdictions for which corporate tax revenues are available in the database, and the share of these revenues as a percentage of gross domestic product (GDP) was 3.2% on average.
- The size of corporate tax revenues relative to total tax revenues and relative to GDP varies by groupings of jurisdictions. In 2021, corporate tax revenues were a larger share of total tax revenues on average in Africa (18.7% in the 32 jurisdictions), Asia and Pacific (18.2% in the 31 jurisdictions) and Latin American and The Caribbean (LAC) (15.4% in the 27 jurisdictions) than the OECD (10.2%). In general, middle and low-income countries are more strongly reliant on corporate income tax as a share of total taxation.
- However, there is less variation between groupings in terms of corporate tax revenues as a share of GDP. The average of corporate tax revenues as a share of GDP was the largest in the OECD and LAC (27 jurisdictions) (3.3% respectively), followed by Asia and Pacific (3.2%) and Africa (2.7%).
- In seventeen jurisdictions – Bhutan, Chad, Cuba, Democratic Republic Of The Congo, Egypt, Equatorial Guinea, Guyana, Hong Kong (China), Indonesia, Kazakhstan, Malaysia, Nigeria, Papua New Guinea, Peru, Singapore, Timor-Leste and Trinidad And Tobago – corporate tax revenues made up more than a quarter of total tax revenues in 2021.

Data on corporate income tax (CIT) revenues can be used for comparison across jurisdictions and to track trends over time. The data in the *Corporate Tax Statistics* database is drawn from the OECD's Global Revenue Statistics Database and allows for the comparison between individual jurisdictions as well as between average corporate tax revenues across OECD, LAC, African, and Asian and Pacific jurisdictions.[1]

The *Corporate Tax Statistics* database contains four corporate tax revenue indicators:

- the level of CIT revenues in national currency;
- the level of CIT tax revenues in USD;
- CIT revenues as a percentage of total tax revenue;
- CIT revenues as a percentage of GDP.

The data are from the OECD's Global Revenue Statistics Database, which presents detailed, internationally comparable data on tax revenues. The classification of taxes and methodology is described in detail in the OECD's Revenue Statistics Interpretative Guide.

Trends in corporate tax revenues

Data from the OECD's *Corporate Tax Statistics* database show that there was an increase in both the average of CIT revenues as a share of total tax revenues and as a share of GDP between 2000 and 2021 across the 123 jurisdictions for which data are available.[2] Average CIT revenues as a share of total tax revenues increased from 12.5% in 2000 to 16.0% in 2021, and average CIT revenues as a percentage of GDP increased from 2.6% in 2000 to 3.2% in 2021.

Between 2000 and 2021, the trend for both indicators is very similar (Figure 1.1). When measured both as a percentage of total tax revenues and as a percentage of GDP, corporate tax revenues reached their peak in 2008 and then dipped in 2009 and 2010, reflecting the impact of the global financial and economic crisis. While average CIT revenues recovered after 2010, the unweighted average across all 123 jurisdictions for which data are available declined in 2014, 2015 and 2016. The unweighted average recovered slightly in 2017, 2018 and 2019 as a result of increases across a wide range of jurisdictions. This was followed by a slight decline in 2020 in both indicators, however in 2021, average CIT revenues as a share of total tax revenues and as a share of GDP both increased and approach levels similar to the peak in 2008.

Figure 1.1. Average corporate tax revenues as a percentage of total tax and as a percentage of GDP

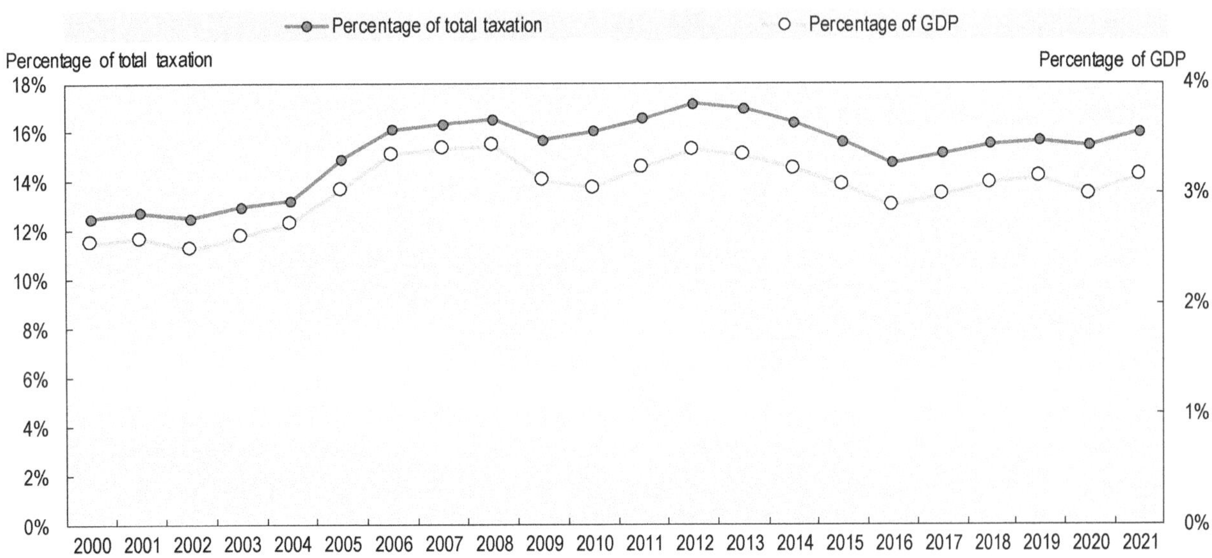

StatLink https://stat.link/cn178d

The averages mask considerable differences across jurisdictions (Figure 1.2). In Bhutan, Chad, Cuba, Democratic Republic Of The Congo, Egypt, Equatorial Guinea, Guyana, Hong Kong (China), Indonesia, Kazakhstan, Malaysia, Nigeria, Papua New Guinea, Peru, Singapore, Timor-Leste and Trinidad And Tobago, CIT revenue accounted for more than 25% of total tax revenue. In Bhutan, Equatorial Guinea, Malaysia and Timor-Leste, it accounted for more than 40%. In contrast, some jurisdictions – such as the Bahamas, Estonia, Greece, Hungary, Italy, Latvia, Nauru, Tokelau and Vanuatu[3] – raised less than 5% of total tax revenue from the CIT. In most jurisdictions, the difference in the level of corporate taxes as a share of total tax revenues reflects differences in the levels of other taxes raised.

The average revenue share of corporate tax in 2021 also varied across the OECD and the regional groupings (LAC, Asia and Pacific and Africa). In 2021, the OECD average was the lowest, at 10.2%, followed by the LAC average (15.4% in 27 jurisdictions), the Asia and Pacific average (18.2% in 31 jurisdictions) and the Africa average (18.7% in 32 jurisdictions).

Some of the variation in the share of CIT in total tax revenues results from differences in statutory corporate tax rates, which also vary considerably across jurisdictions. In addition, this variation can be explained by institutional and jurisdiction-specific factors, including:

- the degree to which firms in a jurisdiction are incorporated;
- the breadth of the CIT base;
- the current stage of the economic cycle and the degree of cyclicality of the corporate tax system (for example, from the generosity of loss offset provisions);
- the extent of reliance on other types of taxation, such as taxes on personal income and on consumption;
- the extent of reliance on tax revenues from the exploitation of natural resources;
- other instruments that postpone the taxation of earned profits.

Generally, differences in corporate tax revenues as a share of total tax revenues should not be interpreted as being related to base erosion and profit shifting (BEPS) behaviour, since many other factors are likely to be more significant, although profit shifting may have some effects at the margin.

Corporate tax revenues as a share of GDP

Corporate tax revenues as a percentage of GDP also vary across jurisdictions. In 2021, the ratio of corporate tax revenues to GDP were between 2% and 5% for a majority of the 123 jurisdictions covered (Figure 1.3). For 12 jurisdictions, corporate tax revenues accounted for more than 5% of GDP. In contrast, they were less than 2% of GDP in 27 jurisdictions. In 2021, the OECD and LAC, and Asia and Pacific averages were similar, at 3.3%, 3.3%, and 3.2% of GDP respectively, whereas the Africa average was lower (2.7%).

The reasons for the variation across jurisdictions in corporate tax revenues as a percentage of GDP are similar to those that explain why the corporate tax revenue share of total tax revenue differs, such as differences in statutory corporate tax rates and differences in the degree to which firms in a given jurisdiction are incorporated. In addition, the total level of taxation as a share of GDP plays a role. For example, for the 32 African jurisdictions, the relatively high average revenue share of CIT compared to the relatively low average of CIT as a percentage of GDP reflects the low amount of total tax raised as a percentage of GDP (average of 15.6%). Total tax revenue as a percentage of GDP is somewhat higher for the 27 LAC jurisdictions (average of 21.7%), the 31 Asian and Pacific jurisdictions (average of 19.8%) and significantly higher for the OECD jurisdictions (average of 34.2%). Across the jurisdictions in the database, low tax-to-GDP ratios may reflect policy choices as well as challenges associated with domestic resource mobilisation (e.g., administrative capacity and levels of compliance). The fact that CIT-to-GDP ratios are similar across countries with varying levels of economic development suggests that variation in total tax-to-GDP ratios is driven more strongly by other tax categories (e.g. PIT, SSCs) than by CIT.

Figure 1.2. Corporate tax revenues as a percentage of total tax revenues, 2021

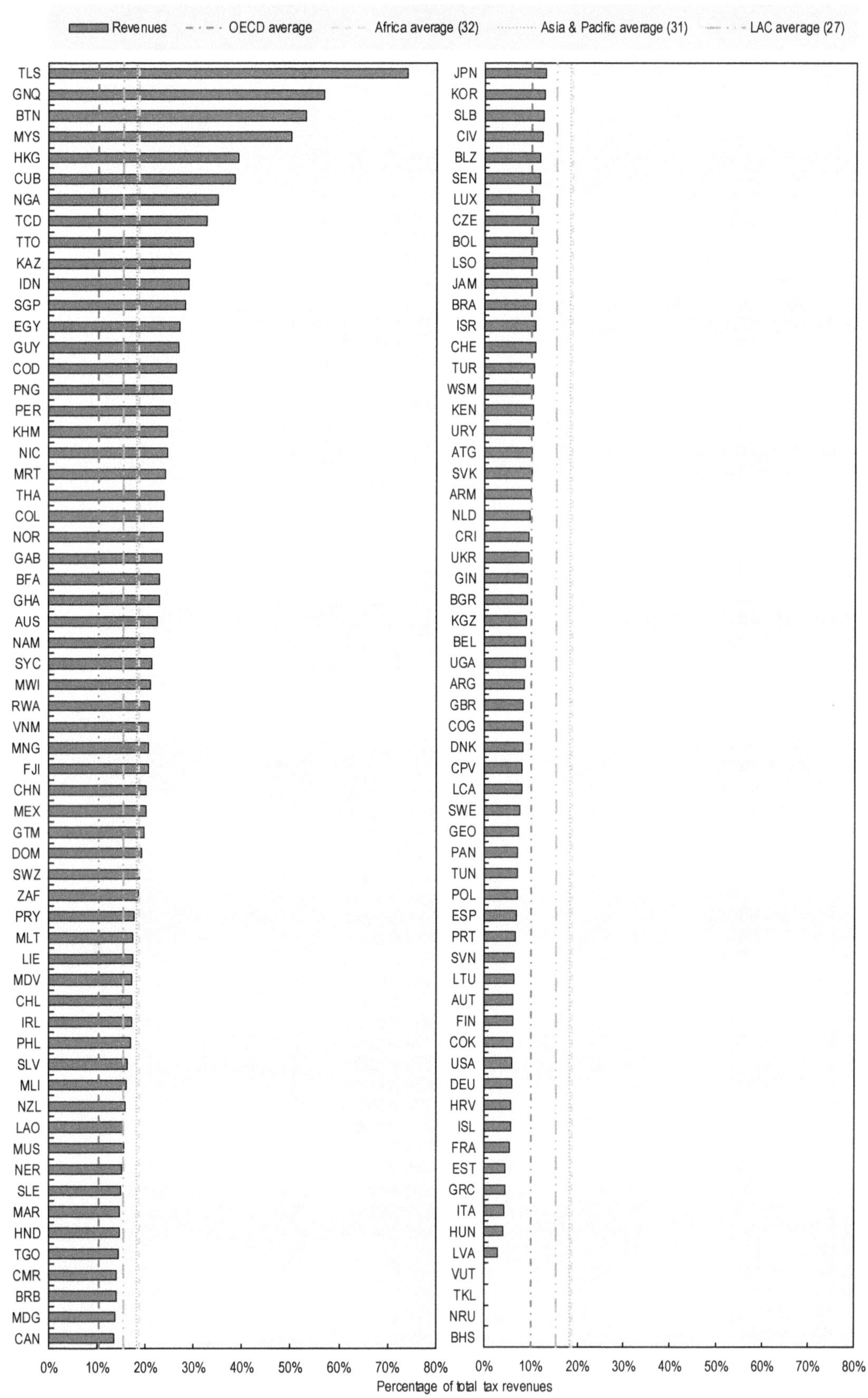

StatLink https://stat.link/l6bc52

Figure 1.3. Corporate tax revenues as a percentage of GDP, 2021

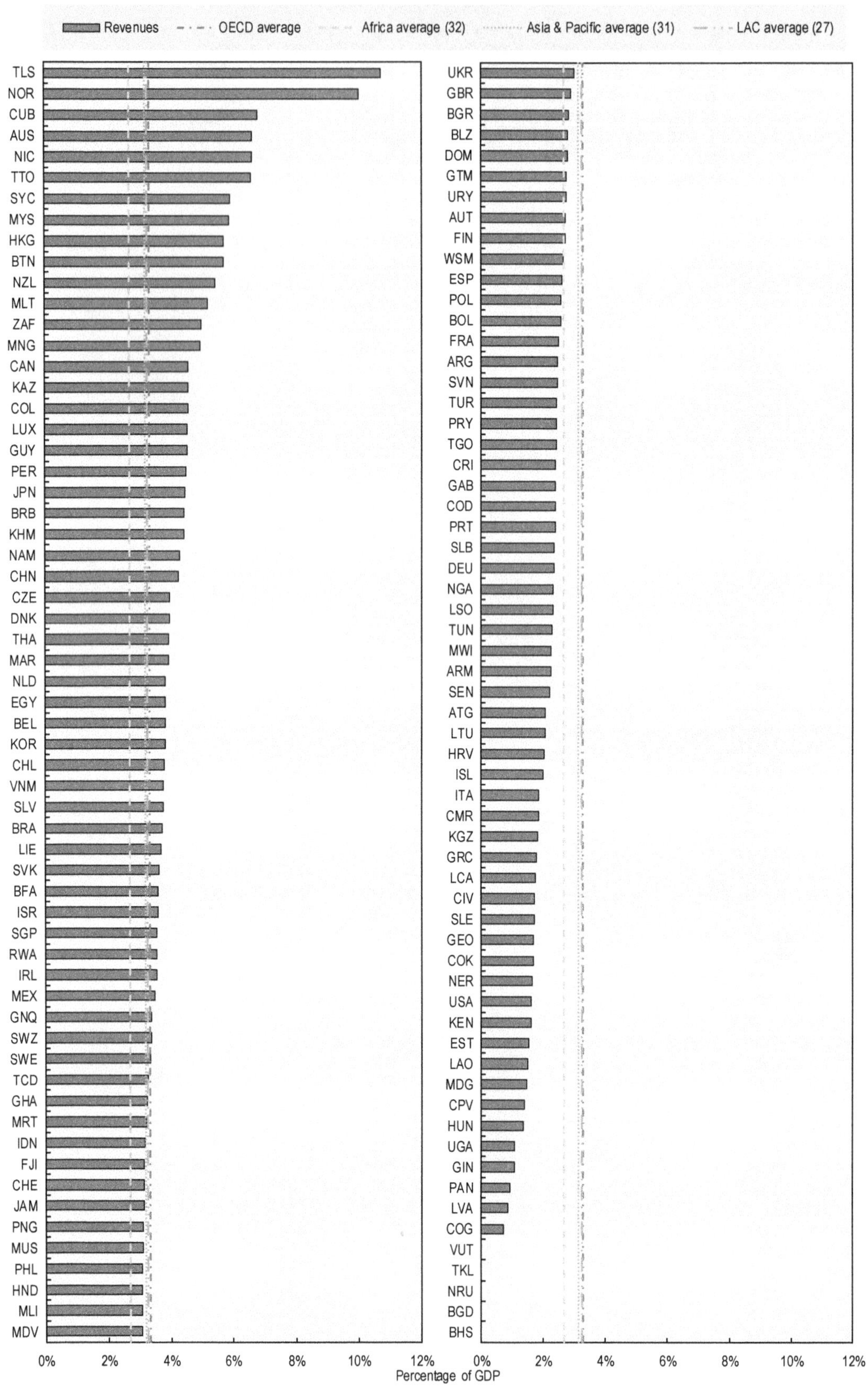

StatLink https://stat.link/sux05w

Notes

[1] The Global Revenue Statistics Database covers 127 jurisdictions as of June 2024. Data on CIT revenues is available for 123 of these jurisdictions. In addition to the OECD, the Global Revenue Statistics Database also contains data on 31 Asian and Pacific jurisdictions, 27 Latin America and Caribbean jurisdictions, and 32 African jurisdictions, and averages for the LAC, African, and Asian and Pacific regions.

[2] The latest tax revenue data available across all jurisdictions in the database are for 2021, although there are 2022 data available for some jurisdictions in the Global Revenue Statistics database.

[3] The Bahamas, Nauru, Tokelau and Vanuatu do not levy a corporate income tax.

2 Statutory corporate income tax rates

Key insights

- Statutory corporate income tax rates (STRs) have remained stable in the period between 2021 and 2024, arresting their long-term decline over the last two decades, though rates remain far below historic averages. The average combined (central and sub-central government) STR for all Inclusive Framework jurisdictions covered declined dramatically from 28.0% in 2000 to 21.7% in 2019. From 2019 to 2024, the average STR has remained relatively stable with a rate of 21.7% in 2019 and 21.1% in 2024.
- Of the 143 jurisdictions covered in the 2024 data, 25 had STRs equal to or above 30% in 2024, with Colombia and Malta having the highest STR at 35.0%.
- In 2024, 11 jurisdictions had no corporate tax regime or an STR of zero. Three jurisdictions, Barbados, Hungary and the United Arab Emirates (all 9%), had a positive STR of less than 10%. Hungary, however, also has a local business tax, which does not use corporate profits as its base. This is not included in Hungary's STR, but it does mean that businesses in Hungary are subject to a higher level of tax than its statutory rate reflects.
- Comparing STRs between 2000 and 2024, 113 jurisdictions had lower tax rates in 2024, while 14 jurisdictions had the same tax rate, and 16 had higher tax rates.
- The largest increases between 2000 and 2024 were in Benin (30 percentage points (p.p.)) and Togo (27 p.p.). Benin and Togo did not previously have a corporate tax regime and introduced one during this time period.
- Comparing 2000 and 2024, 13 jurisdictions – Aruba, Barbados, Belize, Bosnia and Herzegovina, Bulgaria, Democratic Republic of the Congo, Germany, Gibraltar, Guernsey, India, Isle of Man, Jersey and Paraguay – decreased their corporate tax rates by 20 p.p. or more. During this time, Guernsey, Jersey and the Isle of Man eliminated preferential regimes and reduced their standard corporate tax rates to zero and Barbados reduced its standard corporate tax rate to 9.0% after eliminating its preferential regime.
- From 2023 to 2024, the STR decreased in two jurisdictions (Austria and St. Kitts and Nevis) and there were five increases across the 143 jurisdictions covered (Aruba, Barbados, Czechia, Iceland and the United Arab Emirates). The United Arab Emirates did not previously have a corporate tax regime and introduced one from 2024.
- The jurisdiction with the largest decrease in the STR between 2023 and 2024 was St. Kitts and Nevis (8 p.p.).

Statutory corporate income tax rates (STRs) show the headline tax rate faced by corporations and can be used to compare the standard tax rate on corporations across jurisdictions and over time. STRs measure the marginal tax that would be paid on an additional unit of income, in the absence of other provisions in the tax code, they are often used in studies of base erosion and profit shifting (BEPS) to measure the incentive that firms have to shift income between jurisdictions.

STRs, however, do not give a full picture of the tax rates faced by corporations in a given jurisdiction. The STR does not reflect any special regimes or rates targeted to certain industries or income types, nor does it take into account the breadth of the corporate base to which the rate applies. Further information, such as the data on effective corporate tax rates and intellectual property (IP) regimes in the *Corporate Tax Statistics* database, is needed to form a more complete picture of the tax burden on corporations across jurisdictions.

The *Corporate Tax Statistics* database reports STRs for resident corporations at the:

- central government level;
- central government level exclusive of any surtaxes;
- central government level less deductions for subnational taxes;
- sub-central government level;
- combined (central and sub-central) government level.

The standard rate, which is not targeted at any particular industries or income type, is reported. The top marginal rate is reported if a jurisdiction has a progressive corporate tax system. Other special corporate taxes that are levied on a base other than corporate profits are not included.

Most of the downward movement in STRs between 2000 and 2024 was to tax rates equal to or greater than 10% and less than 30% (Figure 2.2). The number of jurisdictions with tax rates equal to or greater than 10% and less than 30% almost tripled from 39 jurisdictions to 104 jurisdictions, and the number of jurisdictions with tax rates equal to or greater than 10% and less than 20% more than quadrupled, from eight to 32 jurisdictions. Of the 143 jurisdictions covered in the 2024 data, 25 had corporate tax rates equal to or above 30% in 2024, with Colombia and Malta having the highest corporate tax rate at 35.0%.[1]

Despite the general downward movement in tax rates during this period, the number of jurisdictions with very low STRs of less than 10% remained fairly stable between 2000 and 2024. There were 16 jurisdictions with STRs of less than 10% in 2000, and 14 below that threshold in 2024.

There has, however, been some movement of jurisdictions into and out of this category, and these movements illustrate how headline STRs do not give a complete picture of the tax burden in a jurisdiction. Between 2005 and 2009, the British Virgin Islands, Guernsey, Jersey[2] and the Isle of Man all moved from corporate tax rates above 10% to zero corporate tax rates. In all of these cases, however, before changing their standard corporate tax rate to zero, they had operated broadly applicable special regimes that resulted in very low tax rates for qualifying companies. Meanwhile, Andorra and the Maldives instituted corporate tax regimes and moved from zero rates to positive tax rates (10% in Andorra beginning in 2012 and 15% in the Maldives beginning in 2011). However, they also introduced preferential regimes as part of their corporate tax systems that offer lower rates to qualifying companies.[3]

Figure 2.1. Statutory corporate income tax rates, 2024

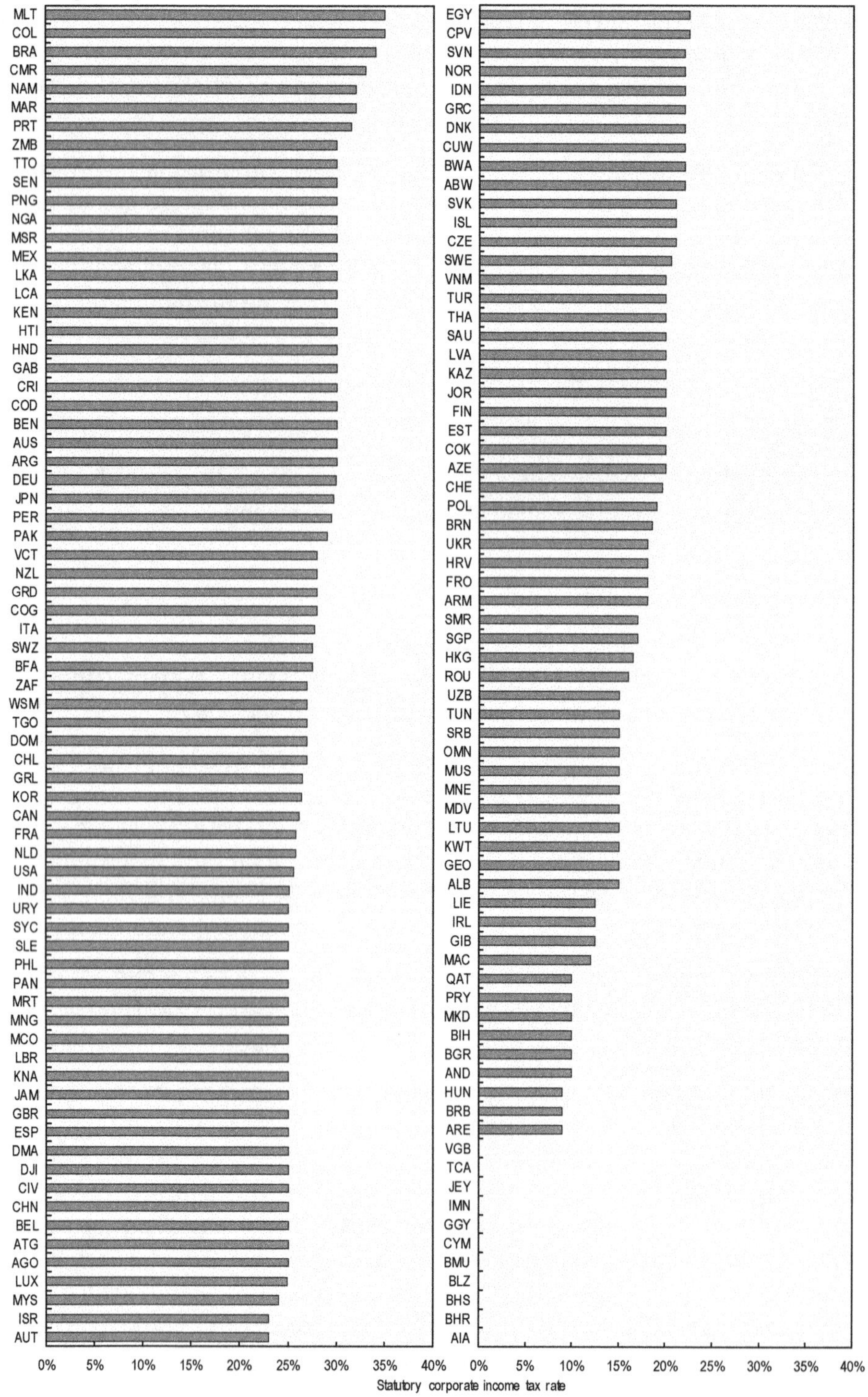

Note: The Kingdom of Saudi Arabia imposes a corporate income tax rate of 20% on a non-Saudi's' share of a resident company or a non-resident's income from a permanent establishment in Saudi Arabia or income of a company operating in the natural gas sector. A higher corporate income tax rate is imposed as well on companies operating in the oil sector (i.e., 50% or higher). The Kingdom of Saudi Arabia also levies the Zakat on companies, which is an example of a tax on both income and equity. The Zakat is levied at 2.5% on a Saudi's share of a resident company (also applies to citizens of Gulf Cooperation Council countries with an established business in the Kingdom of Saudi Arabia), but since it is imposed on income and equity, it yields a higher rate in effective terms. The Saudi government considers the corporate Zakat as an equivalent to corporate income tax, levied on a different basis. It is also considered a covered tax for the purposes of the GloBE rules in the GloBE Model Rules (OECD, 2021[1]) and Commentary.

StatLink https://stat.link/sbmte4

Figure 2.2. Changing distribution of statutory corporate income tax rates

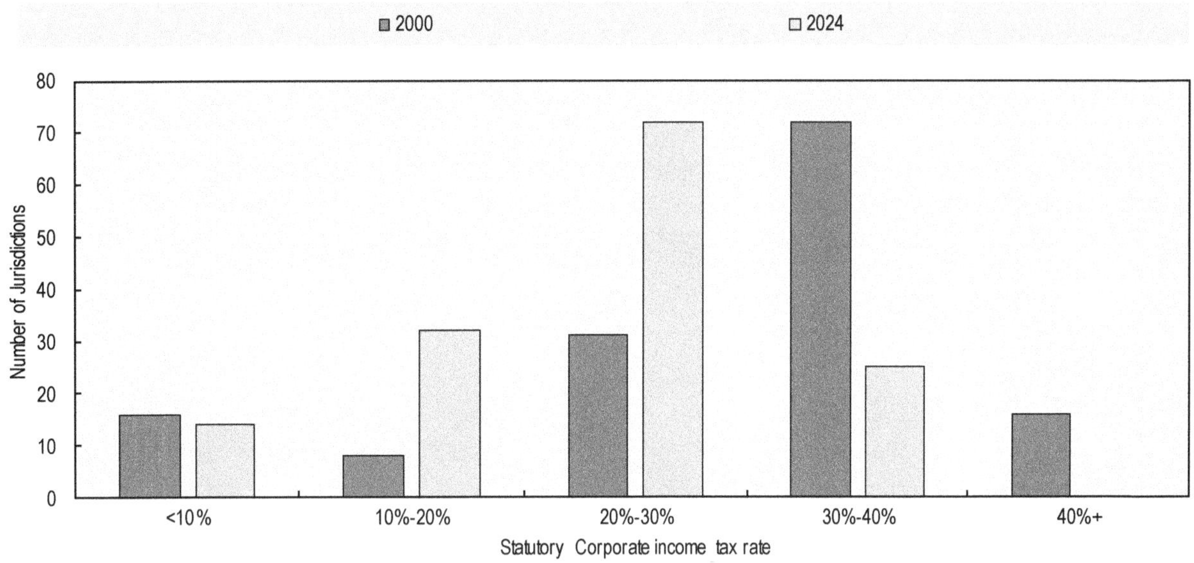

StatLink https://stat.link/a62l0m

Corporate tax rate trends across regions

Since 2000, average STRs have declined across OECD member states and the three regional groupings jurisdictions considered: African jurisdictions, Asian and Pacific jurisdictions and Latin American and The Caribbean (LAC) jurisdictions Figure 2.3.[4]

The grouping with the most significant decline in the average STR has been OECD members (a decline of 8.6 p.p., from 32.3% in 2000 to 23.7% in 2024) followed by LAC with a decline of 5.7 p.p. in 35 jurisdictions, from 26.8% in 2000 to 21.1% in 2024. While the averages have fallen for each grouping over this period, significant differences between the averages for each group remain: the average STR for Africa was 26.5% in 27 jurisdictions in 2024, compared to 23.7% for OECD members, 21.1% in 35 jurisdictions for LAC and 20.4% for 35 jurisdictions in Asia and Pacific.

Recent years have seen a stabilisation of STRs across most of jurisdiction groups covered. From 2019 to 2024, the average STR across all jurisdictions covered has remained relatively stable with a rate of 21.7% in 2019 and 21.1% in 2024. Similarly, there have been declines of only 1.2% in Africa, 0.4% in Asia, 1.1% in LAC, and 0.2% in the OECD.

Over the same period (2019-2024), there have been 14 jurisdictions who have increased their STR, while 29 countries have decreased their rate. In 2023, there were 5 jurisdictions who increased their rate, while 4 jurisdictions decreased their rate. The inclusion of jurisdictions with STRs of zero affects the average tax rate and has larger effects on some regions than on others, since zero rate jurisdictions are not evenly distributed among the different groups. Excluding zero-rate jurisdictions raises the overall average STR by about 1.6 p.p. per year, while the general trends remain the same (see Figure 2.4). From 2000 to 2024, the overall average statutory rate for non-zero rate jurisdictions declined from 29.6% to 22.9%, with some stabilisation in more recent years.

The effect of excluding zero-rate jurisdictions varies by grouping. There are no zero-rate jurisdictions in the OECD or amongst the 27 African jurisdictions, and so the average STRs of these groupings are not affected. However, one of the 35 Asian and Pacific jurisdictions and seven of the 35 LAC jurisdictions have statutory corporate tax rates set at zero. Excluding zero-rate jurisdictions therefore has the largest effect on the average ETR of the LAC region. In 2024, the average STR across all 35 LAC jurisdictions (21.1%)

was 5.3 p.p. lower than the average STR for the 28 LAC jurisdictions with positive CIT rates (26.4%). With the exclusion of zero-rate jurisdictions, the average of the remaining 28 LAC jurisdictions is higher than the OECD average and is almost the same as the average statutory rate for the 27 African jurisdictions.

Figure 2.3. Average statutory corporate income tax rates by region

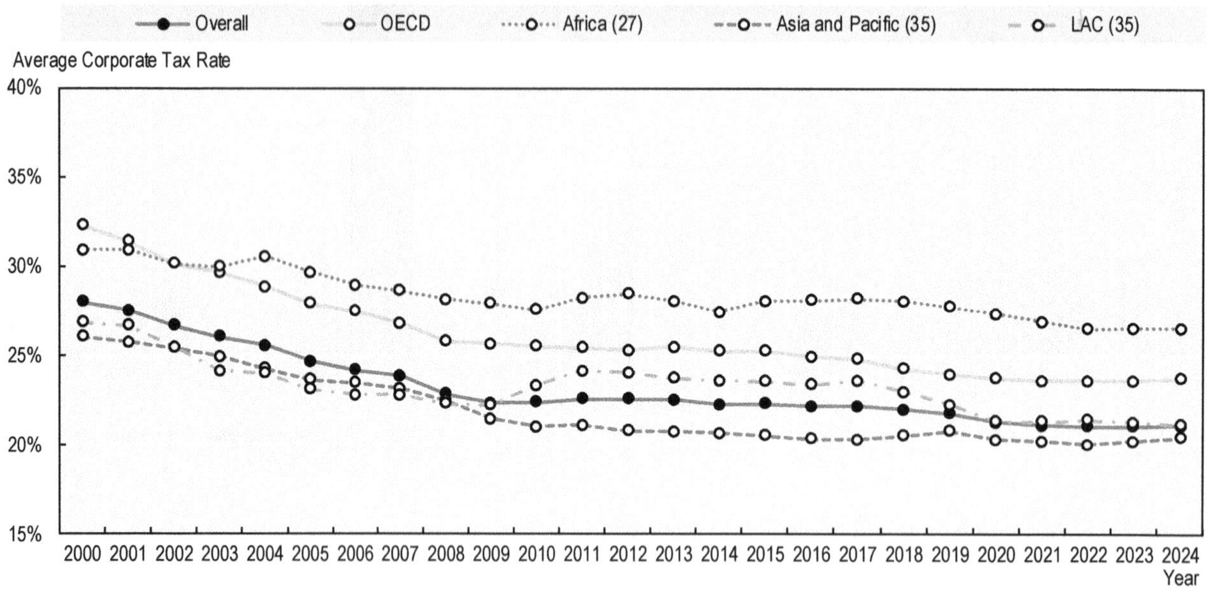

StatLink https://stat.link/xzwamc

Figure 2.4. Average statutory corporate income tax rates by region excluding zero-rate jurisdictions

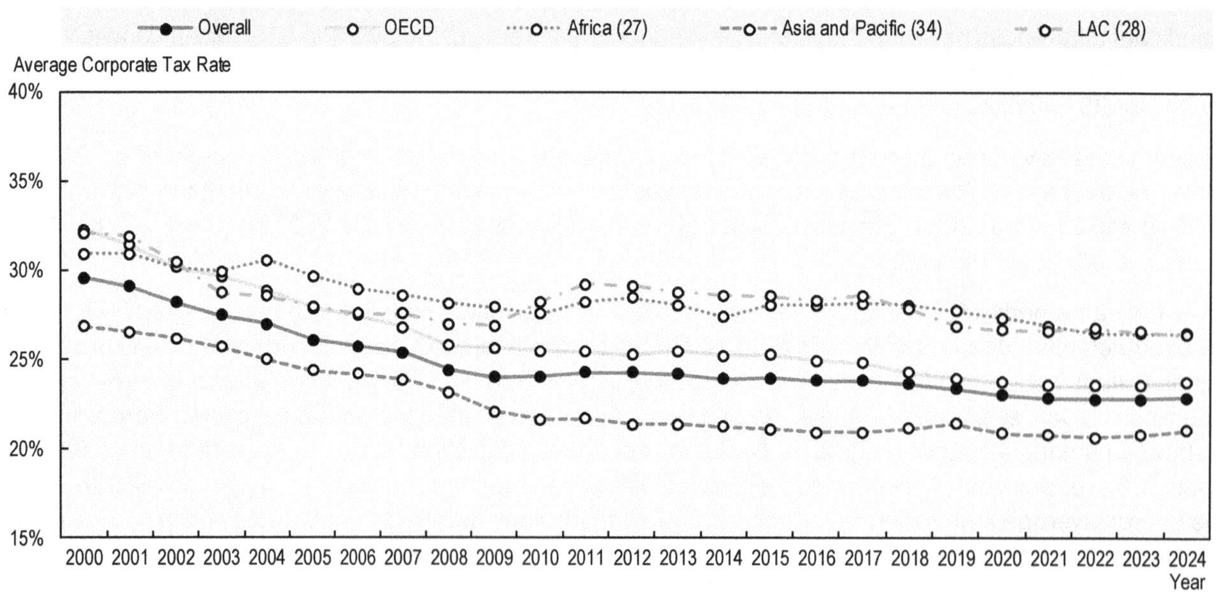

StatLink https://stat.link/x3cqj8

The standard statutory corporate income tax rate is not the only corporate tax rate

Standard STRs provide a snapshot of the corporate tax rate in a jurisdiction. However, jurisdictions may have multiple tax rates with the applicable tax rate depending on the characteristics of the corporation and the income.

- Some jurisdictions operate preferential tax regimes with lower rates offered to certain corporations or income types.
- Some jurisdictions tax retained and distributed earnings at different rates.
- Some jurisdictions impose different tax rates on certain industries.
- Some jurisdictions have progressive rate structures or different regimes for small and medium sized companies.
- Some jurisdictions impose different tax rates on non-resident companies than on resident companies.
- Some jurisdictions impose lower tax rates in special or designated economic zones.

Jurisdictions with broadly applicable tax regimes available to international companies

Preferential tax regimes are especially important in understanding how standard STRs do not always capture the incentives that may exist to engage in BEPS behaviours. In particular, some jurisdictions offer or have offered very low rates through regimes that are available to international companies with relatively few restrictions, while maintaining high standard STRs (OECD, 2022[2]).

For example, a number of jurisdictions offer or have offered International Business Companies regimes. Companies qualifying for these regimes pay a reduced rate of tax relative to the standard STR. While that standard STR may be quite high in these jurisdictions, qualifying international business companies were typically exempt from tax or paid tax at a very low rate. There are also special cases, like Malta, which offers a refund of up to six-sevenths of corporate income taxes to both resident and non-resident investors through its imputation system.

Except for the Maltese imputation system, which is not in the scope of the BEPS project, all of the regimes belonging to jurisdictions for which STR data is available in the *Corporate Tax Statistics* database have been, or are in the process of being, amended or abolished to be aligned with the BEPS Action 5 minimum standard. These changes should greatly diminish the incentives these regimes provide for BEPS behaviour.

Taxes on distributed earnings

Another way in which standard STRs may not reflect the rates imposed on companies is if jurisdictions tax distributed earnings in addition to (or instead of) a CIT on all profits.

In some jurisdictions, there is a tax on all corporate profits when they are earned and an additional tax on any earnings that are distributed. This was the case in India, for example, where corporate profits, whether retained or distributed, were taxed at the standard rate, and an additional tax on dividend distributions raised the total tax rate on distributed profits. From 2020 companies are no longer subject to this dividend distribution tax which has led to a large reduction in the STR from 40.6% in 2019 to 25.2% in 2024.

In other jurisdictions, there is no tax on profits when they are earned, and corporate tax is only imposed when profits are distributed. This is the case in Estonia and Latvia, which both tax distributed profits at 20% and impose no tax on retained earnings. While a standard STR of 20% is reported for both jurisdictions in the *Corporate Tax Statistics* database, the rate faced by corporations in these jurisdictions could be much lower and will depend on the proportion of profits that are distributed. In the case of both of these jurisdictions, where a corporation retains all profits and does not pay any dividends in a given period, it will not be subject to any CIT.

References

OECD (2022), *OECD Investment Tax Incentives Database – 2022 Update: Tax incentives for sustainable development (brochure)*, OECD Publishing, Paris, https://www.oecd.org/investment/investment-policy/oecd-investment-tax-incentives-database-2022-update-brochure.pdf. [2]

OECD (2021), *Tax Challenges Arising from Digitalisation of the Economy – Global Anti-Base Erosion Model Rules (Pillar Two): Inclusive Framework on BEPS*, OECD/G20 Base Erosion and Profit Shifting Project, OECD Publishing, Paris, https://doi.org/10.1787/782bac33-en. [1]

Notes

[1] However, Malta offers a refund of up to six-sevenths of corporate income taxes to both resident and non-resident investors through its imputation system. The corporate tax rate in Belize is 40% but as this rate applies only to the petroleum industry, the corporate tax rate in Belize has been included in this database as 0% to ensure consistency of treatment across all jurisdictions.

[2] Jersey's current corporate income tax regime offers bands of 0%, and for certain targeted sectors, 10% and 20%.

[3] Andorra and the Maldives have since amended or abolished their preferential regimes that were not compliant with the BEPS Action 5 minimum standard.

[4] As the sample of jurisdictions for which tax revenue data are available and the sample of jurisdictions for which statutory corporate tax rate data are available are not identical, the average corporate tax revenue and STR data for the different regional groups should not be directly compared.

3 Withholding tax rates and tax treaties

Withholding taxes (WHTs) are levied on businesses when they make payments to other foreign or domestic business entities or individuals, e.g., in the form of dividends, interest, and royalties. Governments collect these taxes based on statutory or preferential treaty-based tax rates requiring businesses to withhold a fraction of cross-border payments in scope of the WHT.

Data on withholding taxes can be used to improve understanding of multinational enterprise (MNE) decisions about investment, repatriation, finance and organisational structures among other tax policy issues. For example:

- WHTs increase the cost of repatriating profits earned in foreign jurisdictions thereby potentially discouraging MNEs' investment decisions at the extensive margin (i.e., discrete investment decisions between two or more alternative projects);
- differences in WHT rates between interest and dividend payments, both within and across locations, could affect MNEs' financing decisions;
- taxes levied on cross-border payments increase the cost of capital and could thus affect investments at the intensive margin (i.e., the incentive to expand existing investments given a fixed location). (Auerbach, Devereux and Simpson, 2008[1])

Importantly, WHT data can also potentially provide insights on certain base erosion and profit shifting (BEPS) strategies such as treaty shopping or the strategic location of debt and intangible assets. The publication of WHT rates in *Corporate Tax Statistics* was envisaged in the 2015 BEPS Action 11 Report (OECD, 2015[2]).

General data characteristics

The 2024 edition of *Corporate Tax Statistics* includes the third release of WHT rate statistics. The dataset consists of tax rates on dividends, interest and royalty payments that are applicable as of the 2024 fiscal year. They were collected through a questionnaire completed by delegates of Working Party No.2 meeting in of the Inclusive Framework on BEPS (IF) format. Where necessary, information was completed using public sources of information. In total, the dataset includes 144 jurisdictions, including all Inclusive Framework members. It is important to note that baseline withholding tax rates are often not applicable to cross-border transactions, particularly in cases where a tax treaty is in force between two jurisdictions.

Standard withholding tax rates across jurisdictions

Figure 3.1 displays the average standard withholding tax rates applicable for dividends, interest, and royalty payments across the 144 jurisdictions covered. Jurisdictions are categorised in three groups: high-income jurisdictions, low- and middle-income jurisdictions and investment hubs.[1] Figure 3.1 shows that the ranking of average standard WHT rates varies across jurisdiction groups. On average, low and middle-income jurisdictions levy higher WHT rates on royalty payments while high income jurisdictions and investment hubs levy higher rates on interest. In particular, the following can be observed:

- **Dividends:** High income jurisdictions levy an average standard WHT on dividends of 15.2%, which is 3.0 p.p. larger than the average standard WHT rate on dividends in low and middle-income jurisdictions (12.2%) and about three times larger than the average rate in investment hubs (5.2%).
- **Interest:** Concerning interest payments, the average standard WHT rate in high income jurisdictions is 12.8% compared to 14.9% in low and middle-income jurisdictions and 5.7% in investment hubs.
- **Royalties:** Royalty payments are subject to an average standard WHT rate of 15.6% in high income jurisdictions and 16.4% in low and middle-income jurisdictions. These rates are considerably higher than the average standard 5.7% WHT rate applied to royalties in investment hubs.

Figure 3.1. Average withholding tax rates: Dividends, interest, and royalties, 2024

Investment hubs, low and middle income, and high-income jurisdictions

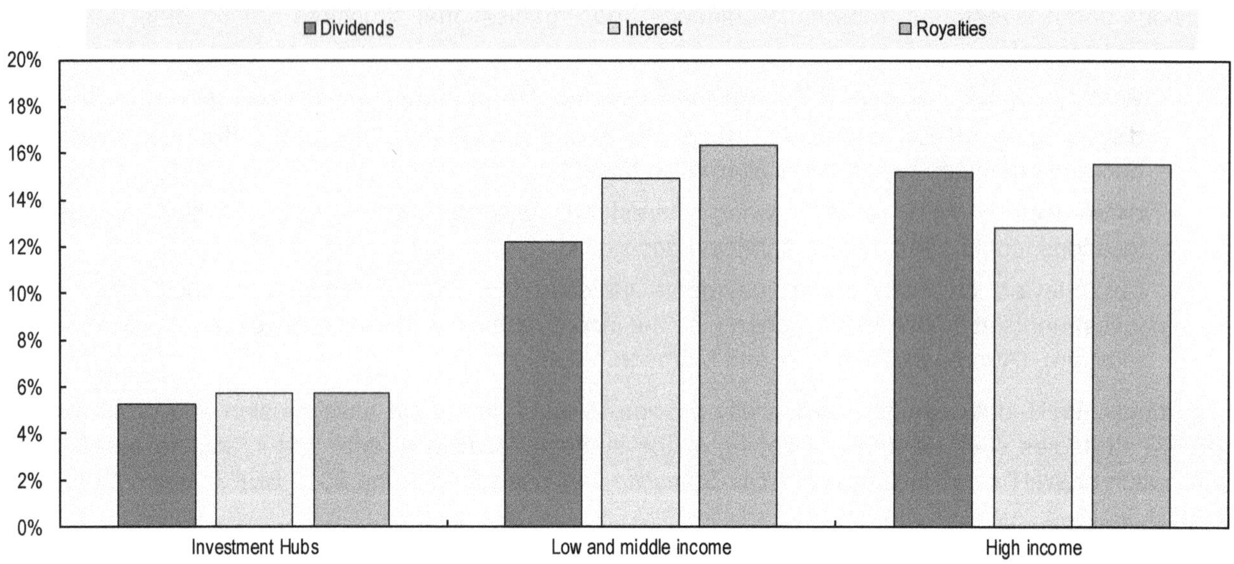

StatLink https://stat.link/4t06wz

Figure 3.2 depicts the density ratios of WHT rates for the three jurisdiction groups along four ranges of WHT rates. Density ratios capture the number of jurisdictions that levy a standard WHT rate in each range, as a share (expressed in p.p.) of the total number of jurisdictions in the dataset. Ratios are presented separately for each jurisdiction group as well as for each cross-border payment type. Panel A of Figure 3.2 shows the distribution of ratios for WHTs on cross-border dividend payments. Almost three quarters (71%) of the investment hubs covered in the dataset levy a WHT on dividends at a standard rate below 10%. This includes, among others, Anguilla (0.0%), Cyprus (0.0%), and Singapore (0.0%). Nineteen per cent of investment hubs levy a WHT on dividends at a standard rate between 10% and 20%. The remaining jurisdictions are Ireland and Switzerland, which levy a WHT on dividends at standard rates of 25.0%.

Among low and middle-income jurisdictions, more than half levy a WHT on dividends at a standard rate between 10% and 20%. Fifteen of the 68 jurisdictions in this group have standard WHT rates below 10%, including Brazil (0.0%) and Peru (5.0%). Of the low and middle-income jurisdictions, only Jamaica (33.3%) has a standard WHT rate on dividends above 30%. The largest share of high-income jurisdictions (about one third) levy WHTs on dividends at standard rates below 10%. This includes the United Kingdom (0.0%), Greece (5.0%), and Uruguay (7.0%), among others. In the remaining three ranges of standard WHT rates above 10%, the number of high-income jurisdictions is between 11 and 13 jurisdictions for each range. At the top-end of the distribution are jurisdictions such as Chile (35.0%), Czechia (35.0%), and Greenland (44.0%). As mentioned above, these rates do not account for any tax treaties that may exist.

Figure 3.2. Density ratios of WHT rates: Dividends, interest, and royalties, 2024

Investment hubs, low and middle income, and high-income countries

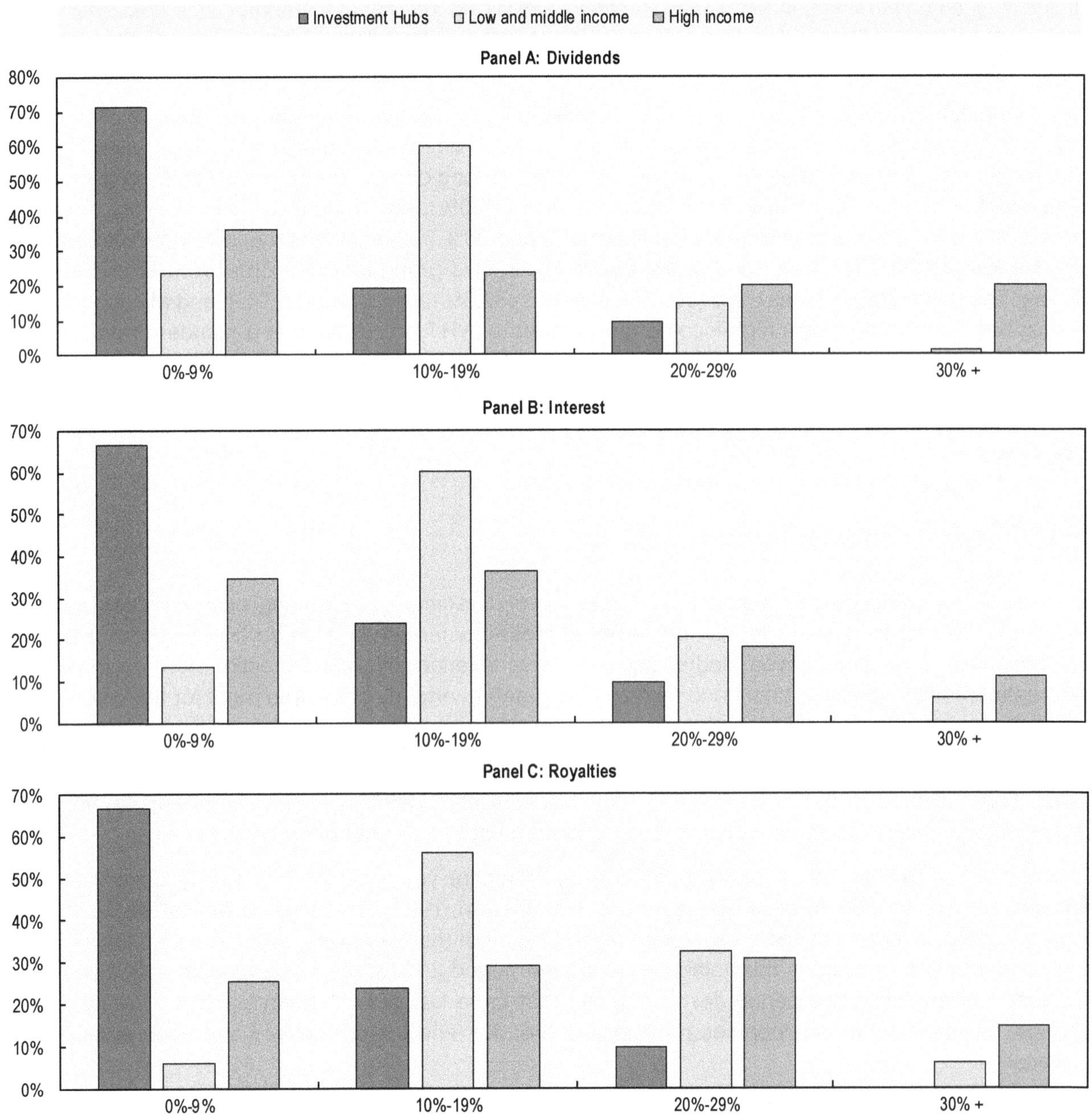

StatLink https://stat.link/8nb674

Panel B of Figure 3.2 presents the spread of density ratios applicable to cross-border interest payments. The majority of investment hubs (67% of the group) levy a WHT on interest at a standard rate below 10%. Among others, this includes Malta (0.0%) and the Netherlands (0.0%). Of the remaining seven investment hubs, Switzerland (25.0%) and Ireland (20%) are at the top of the distribution of standard rates. 59% of low and middle-income jurisdictions levy a WHT on interest at a standard rate between 10% and 20%.

Eight jurisdictions levy a WHT on interest at a standard rate lower than 10%, including Paraguay (4.5%), Georgia (5.0%), and Viet Nam (5.0%). Four jurisdictions levy a WHT on interest at a rate greater than 30% including Peru (30.0%), Jamaica (33.3%), Argentina (35.0%) and Mexico (35.0%). High income jurisdictions are concentrated in the lower parts of the distribution, with 34.5% of high-income jurisdictions levying WHTs on interest at standard rates below 10%. In the higher tax brackets, 36.4% of jurisdictions levy WHTs on interest at standard rates between 10% and 20%, 18.2% between 20 and 30% group, and 10.9% above 30%. Liechtenstein (0.0%), Monaco (0.0%) and Sweden (0.0%) are three of the 55 jurisdictions among the high-income group that levy a WHT on interest at a standard rate below 10%. The highest standard WHT rate among high income jurisdictions is levied at the same rate (35.0%) in Chile, Czechia and the Slovak Republic.

The distribution of density ratios of WHTs on cross-border royalty payments are found in Panel C of Figure 3.2. Most investment hubs have standard WHT rates on royalties below 10%. This range includes Hungary (0.0%), Jersey (0.0%), and Hong-Kong (5.0%), among others. The upper tail of the distribution of investment hubs consists of Liberia (15.0%), Mauritius (15.0%), and Ireland (20.0%). Royalty payments are subject to WHTs at standard rates between 10% and 20% in over half of the low and middle-income jurisdictions (55.9%). The lower end of the distribution in this group includes Brazil (0.0%) and Georgia (5.0%). The upper end includes Peru (30.0%), Jamaica (33.3%), Argentina (35.0%), and Mexico (35.0%). Almost one third (31%) of the high-income group levies a WHT on royalties at a standard rate between 20% and 30%. Among the high-income jurisdictions that levy the lowest standard WHT rates are Aruba (0.0%), Latvia (0.0%), and the United Arab Emirates (0.0%). Belgium (30.0%), Italy (30.0%), and the United States (30.0%) are three of the eight jurisdictions that levy WHTs at a standard rate of 30% or above in this category.

Treaty-based withholding tax rates

Bilateral tax conventions can play a crucial role in encouraging and fostering economic ties between countries. They do so by reducing tax obstacles to cross-border services, trade and investment through the avoidance of double taxation, addressing excessive taxation, offering protection from discriminatory tax treatment of foreign investment and by providing greater certainty of tax treatment for taxpayers.

One way in which bilateral tax treaties achieve some of these aims is through the limitation of withholding taxes that may be applied certain income. This section provides data on the tax treaties amongst the jurisdictions covered in the database and provides additional details on the withholding tax rates on dividends, interest, royalties, and technical fees, that are applied as final withholding tax rates.[2]

The number of treaties has expanded significantly in recent years across the 144 jurisdictions in the dataset, with only 1008 treaties among these countries in 1990 compared to almost 4850 in 2024 Figure 3.3. However recent years have seen a levelling off of the expansion in tax treaties, with only 294 additional treaties included in the database during the period 2017-2024.[3] The modest increase in new bilateral treaties during this period does not mean that there has not still been significant treaty-related change; for example, many countries have signed the MLI, and many treaties have been amended by protocol.

The data suggest that countries outside the OECD have fewer treaties than OECD countries. Figure 3.4 shows that OECD countries have higher numbers of treaties on average than IF member jurisdictions in Africa and Latin American and the Caribbean, which contain more non-OECD member jurisdictions. Though all groups have seen significant growth in their average number of tax treaties, this growth has been strongest amongst OECD countries. The data show that treaty-based withholding tax rates are substantially lower than withholding tax rates applicable under domestic law. Overall, Figure 3.5 shows that treaty-based withholding tax rates show a substantial mass of rates below 5%.

Figure 3.3. Number of bilateral treaties, 1990-2024

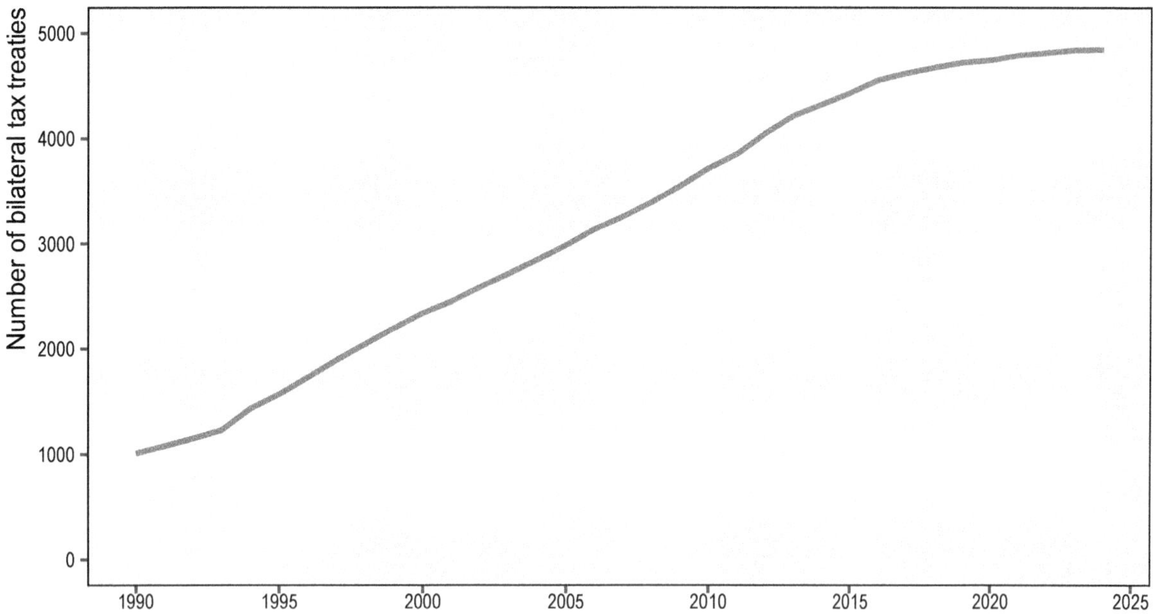

Note: Data are based on bilateral treaties reported by all IF member jurisdictions and one non-IF jurisdiction. The database refers to bilateral tax treaties only. Multilateral agreements are not accounted for. Other tax-related agreements such as tax information exchange agreements are not counted. Only treaties in effect are counted.
Source: OECD Bilateral Tax Treaties Database.

StatLink https://stat.link/dt51a2

Figure 3.4. Average number of treaties, by region

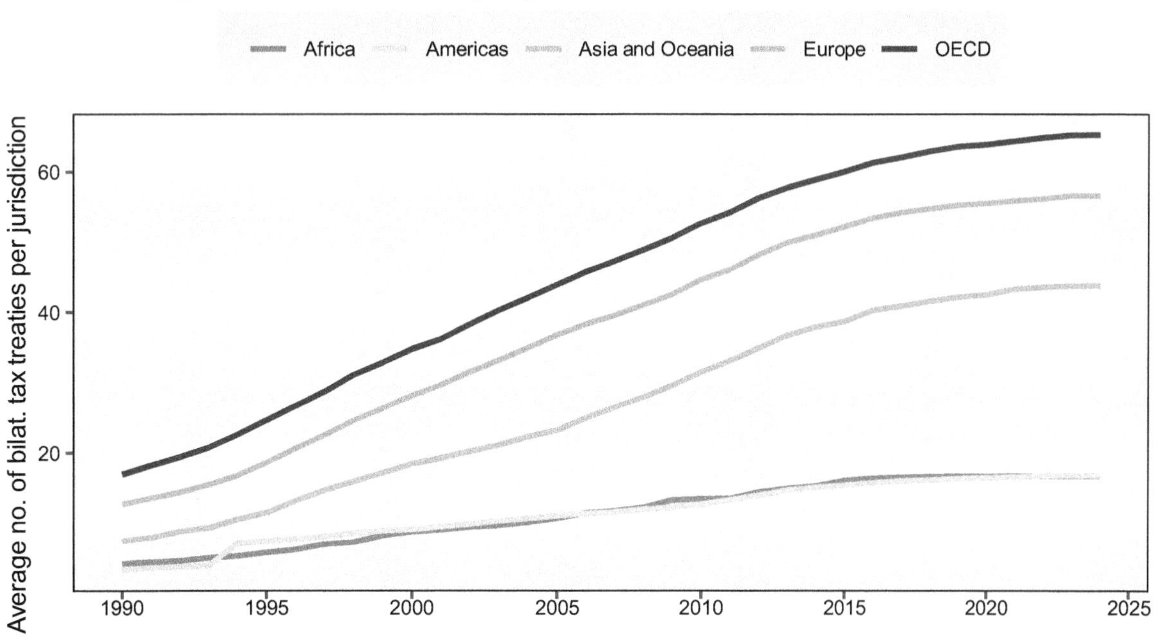

Note: Data are based on bilateral treaties reported by all IF member jurisdictions and one non-IF jurisdiction. The database refers to bilateral tax treaties only. Multilateral agreements are not accounted for. Other tax-related agreements such as tax information exchange agreements are not counted. Only treaties in effect are counted.
Source: OECD Bilateral Tax Treaties Database.

StatLink https://stat.link/3it2p7

Figure 3.5. Average treaty-based withholding tax rates

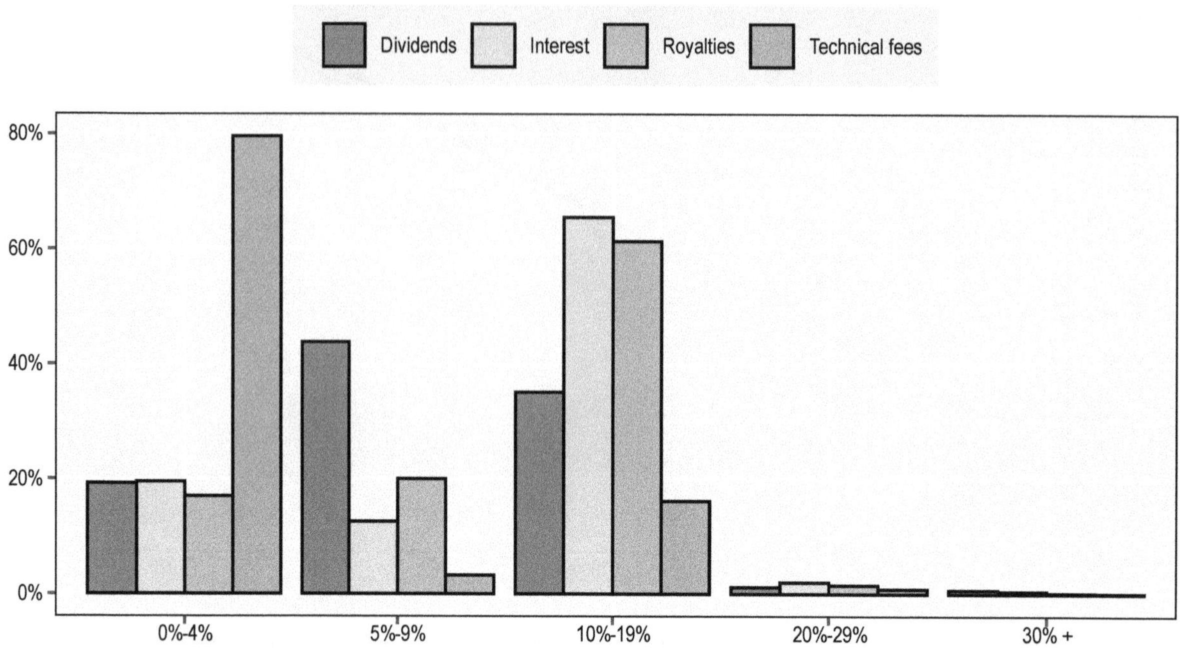

Note: Data are based on bilateral treaties reported by all IF member jurisdictions and one non-IF jurisdiction. The database refers to bilateral tax treaties only. Multilateral agreements are not accounted for. Other tax-related agreements such as tax information exchange agreements are not counted. Only treaties in effect are counted. For each of the categories of payment flows, existing treaties that do not specify the applicable withholding tax rate, and hence create missing values, are not included in this figure. Where a tax treaty provides for different rates for specified ownership percentages, this entry reflects the highest ownership percentage.
Source: OECD Bilateral Tax Treaties Data.

StatLink https://stat.link/385dg7

References

Auerbach, A., M. Devereux and H. Simpson (2008), “Taxing corporate income”, https://www.nber.org/papers/w14494 (accessed on 18 February 2023). [1]

OECD (2015), *Measuring and Monitoring BEPS, Action 11 - 2015 Final Report*, OECD/G20 Base Erosion and Profit Shifting Project, OECD Publishing, Paris, https://doi.org/10.1787/9789264241343-en. [2]

Notes

[1] The “high income” and “low and middle income” jurisdiction groups are based on the World Bank classification, with the resulting split for the 119 jurisdictions covered: 49 high-income jurisdictions and 49 low- and middle-income jurisdictions. Low- and middle-income jurisdictions are grouped together due to the low number of low-income countries (two) in the dataset. Investment hubs constitute the third group. They are defined as jurisdictions with a total inward Foreign Direct Investment (FDI) position above 150% of gross domestic product (GDP) and include 21 jurisdictions.

[2] This means that the payments are not effectively connected with a permanent establishment in a jurisdiction applying a WHT.

[3] The analysis does not include updates or amendments to treaties. The data also do not include bilateral tax instruments that do not amend withholding taxes, such as taxpayer information exchange agreements.

4 Corporate effective tax rates

Key insights

- Of the 90 jurisdictions covered for 2023, 79 provide accelerated depreciation, which results in Effective Average Tax Rate (EATRs) on investments in these jurisdictions below their statutory tax rate (STRs). Among those jurisdictions, the average reduction of the STR was 1.9 p.p.; in 2023, the largest reductions were observed in Mauritius (9.3 p.p.), Italy (6.6 p.p.), Malta, (6.2 p.p.), Nigeria (4.3 p.p.), Poland (4.0 p.p.), and Chile (3.6 p.p.). In contrast, fiscal depreciation was decelerated in five jurisdictions, leading to EATRs above the statutory tax rate. Among those jurisdictions, the average difference between the EATR and the STR was 4.2 p.p.; the largest differences between EATRs and STRs were observed in Botswana (9.3 p.p.), Argentina (4.9 p.p.) and Liberia (4.7 p.p.).
- Among all 90 jurisdictions, eight jurisdictions had an allowance for corporate equity (ACE): Belgium, Cyprus, Italy, Liechtenstein, Malta, Poland, Portugal and Türkiye. Including this provision in their tax code has led to an additional reduction in their EATRs of between 0.3 to 4.5 p.p.
- The average EATR across jurisdictions (20.2%) is 1.0 p.p. lower than the average STR (21.2%). The median EATR is 2.8 p.p. lower (22.2%) than the median STR (25.0%). While more than half of the jurisdictions covered have EATRs between 15% and 28%, several Latin American and The Caribbean (LAC) jurisdictions have EATRs at the higher end of the range due to the decelerating effect of their tax depreciation rules for acquired software (e.g., Colombia and Brazil).
- Effective marginal tax rates (EMTRs) are among the lowest in jurisdictions with an allowance for corporate equity, i.e., Cyprus, Italy, Liechtenstein, Malta, Poland, Portugal and Türkiye.
- Nine jurisdictions have decreased the generosity of their tax depreciation rules, resulting in an increase in their EMTRs in 2023 compared to 2022; the largest increase was observed in Italy (52 p.p.).
- Three jurisdictions have increased the generosity of their tax depreciation rules, leading to lower EMTRs in 2023 than in 2022; this group includes Austria (1.3 p.p.), Korea (1.2 p.p.) and Türkiye (1.0 p.p.).
- Disaggregating the results to the asset level shows that fiscal acceleration is strongest for investments in buildings and tangible assets. The average EATR across jurisdictions is 18.9% for buildings and 19.3% for tangible assets, lower than the average composite EATR (19.6%), which also includes acquired software and inventories. For the tangible asset category, which covers air, railroad and water transport vehicles, road transport vehicles, computer hardware, industrial machinery and equipment, most of this effect is driven by more generous tax depreciation rules for air, railroad and water transport vehicles, as well as for industrial machinery.
- Over recent years, EATRs have remained relatively stable on average, with modest declines at the top and bottom of the distribution across countries. Average EATRs were 20.9% in 2019 and 20.2% in 2023, while median EATRs were 22.9% in 2019 and 22.7% in 2023. This may reflect the stabilisation of STRs discussed in Chapter 2, which are a key component of the EATRs.

- By contrast, the EMTRs have declined over the previous five years, with the average EATR being 19.6% in 2019 and 16.6% in 2023. The stability of EATRs combined with declines in EMTRs suggests a narrowing of tax bases in the sample, notably through an increase in the generosity of depreciation provisions. Examining the asset breakdown shows these trends have been driven by increased generosity of depreciation of tangible and intangible assets, as opposed to buildings and inventories.

Variations in the definition of corporate tax bases across jurisdictions can have a significant impact on the tax liability associated with a given investment. For instance, corporate tax systems differ across jurisdictions with regard to several important features, such as fiscal depreciation rules as well as other tax provisions. To capture the effects of these provisions on corporate tax bases and tax liabilities, it is necessary to go beyond a comparison of statutory corporate income tax (CIT) rates.

The *Corporate Tax Statistics* dataset presents "forward-looking" ETRs, which are synthetic tax policy indicators calculated using information about specific tax policy rules. Unlike "backward-looking" ETRs, they do not incorporate any information about firms' actual tax payments. As described in more detail in Box 4.1, the ETRs reported in *Corporate Tax Statistics* focus on the effects of fiscal depreciation and several related provisions (e.g., allowances for corporate equity, half-year conventions, inventory valuation methods). While this includes fiscal depreciation rules for certain kinds of intangible property, namely acquired software, the effects of expenditure-based R&D tax incentives and intellectual property (IP) regimes are not accounted for in the baseline data discussed in this chapter. However, the following chapter presents forward-looking ETRs capturing the effects of R&D tax incentives on R&D investments.

The *Corporate Tax Statistics* database contains four forward-looking tax policy indicators reflecting tax rules as of 1 July for the years 2017-23:

- the effective average tax rate (EATR);
- the effective marginal tax rate (EMTR);
- the cost of capital;
- the net present value of capital allowances as a share of the initial investment.

All four tax policy indicators are calculated by applying jurisdiction-specific tax rules to a prospective, hypothetical investment project. Calculations are undertaken separately for investments in different asset types and sources of financing (i.e., debt and equity). Composite tax policy indicators are computed by weighting over assets and sources of finance. More disaggregated results are also reported in the *Corporate Tax Statistics* database. This chapter discusses only results for two indicators: the EMTR and the EATR.

The tax policy indicators are calculated for two different macroeconomic scenarios. Unless noted, the results reported in this publication refer to composite effective tax rates based on the macroeconomic scenario with 3% real interest rate and 1% inflation.

Forward-looking corporate effective tax rates in 2023

Two complementary forward-looking ETRs are typically used for tax policy analysis, capturing incentives at different margins of investment decision making:

- EATRs reflect the average tax contribution a firm makes on an investment project earning above-zero economic profits. This indicator is used to analyse discrete investment decisions between two or more alternative projects (along the extensive margin).

- EMTRs measure the extent to which taxation increases the pre-tax rate of return required by investors to break even. This indicator is used to analyse how taxes affect the incentive to expand existing investments given a fixed location (along the intensive margin).

Effective average tax rates

Figure 4.1 shows the composite EATR for the full database. In most jurisdictions, EATRs diverge from the statutory CIT rate; if fiscal depreciation is generous compared to true economic depreciation or if there are other significant base narrowing provisions, the EATR (and also the EMTR) will be lower than the statutory tax rate, i.e., tax depreciation is accelerated. On the other hand, if tax depreciation does not cover the full effects of true economic depreciation, it is decelerated, implying that the tax base will be larger and effective taxation higher.

To allow comparison with the statutory tax rate, the share of the EATR (in p.p.) that is due to a deceleration of the tax base is shaded in light blue in Figure 4.1; reductions of the STR due to acceleration are transparent. In addition, the reduction in the EATR due to an ACE is indicated as a dotted area.

Comparing the patterns of tax depreciation across jurisdictions shows that most jurisdictions provide some degree of acceleration, as indicated by the transparent bars. The most significant effects being observed in jurisdictions with an ACE, such as Italy, Malta, Poland, Portugal and Türkiye among others, as well as in jurisdictions with larger accelerated depreciation provisions, such as Canada, South Africa, the United Kingdom and the United States. While fewer jurisdictions have decelerating tax depreciation rules, the effect of deceleration can become large in jurisdictions where acquired software is non-depreciable (Botswana) or depreciable at a very low rate (e.g., in Argentina and to a lesser extent also in Mexico, Papua New Guinea and Peru).

Between 2017 and 2023, average EATRs have tended to decline modestly. Looking at the development of the composite EATR from 2017 and 2023, the unweighted average composite EATR has declined modestly over this period (1.4 p.p.), from 21.6% in 2017 to 20.2% in 2023. The average STR has declined somewhat less over the same time period (1.0 p.p.), from 22.2% in 2017 to 21.2% in 2023, implying that changes to the corporate tax base have also contributed to the reduction in EATRs as well as reductions in the headline rates.

The distribution of EATRs has shifted slightly downwards between 2017 and 2023. Figure 4.2 shows the evolution of different points of the EATR distribution over time. The median represents the EATR of the jurisdiction that lies in the middle of the distribution, 50% of jurisdictions would have EATRs above this value. The 25th percentile represents the EATR where 25% of the jurisdictions would be below this value, and the 75th represents the EATR where 75% of the jurisdictions would be below this value. The median EATR has remained largely steady over the period, with a rate of 22.8% in 2017 and 22.7% in 2023, while the top and bottom of the distribution have dropped from 27.7% and 17.0% in 2017 to 26.6% and 16.2% in 2023.

Changes to the distribution of the EATR can be attributed to the decline over time in statutory CIT rates and to various base reforms. The largest changes in the distribution of EATRs are concentrated in 2021. In 2021 the median EATR dropped to 22.5%, from 22.8% in 2020 (a decline of 0.3 p.p.). During this year, several countries implemented significant changes in their CIT systems which can explain the observed downward trend. Some of these related to reductions in statutory CIT rates or the introduction of base narrowing. From 2021 to 2023 EATRs have remained largely steady with a value of 20.0% in 2022, and 20.2% in 2023.

Figure 4.1. Effective average tax rates, 2023

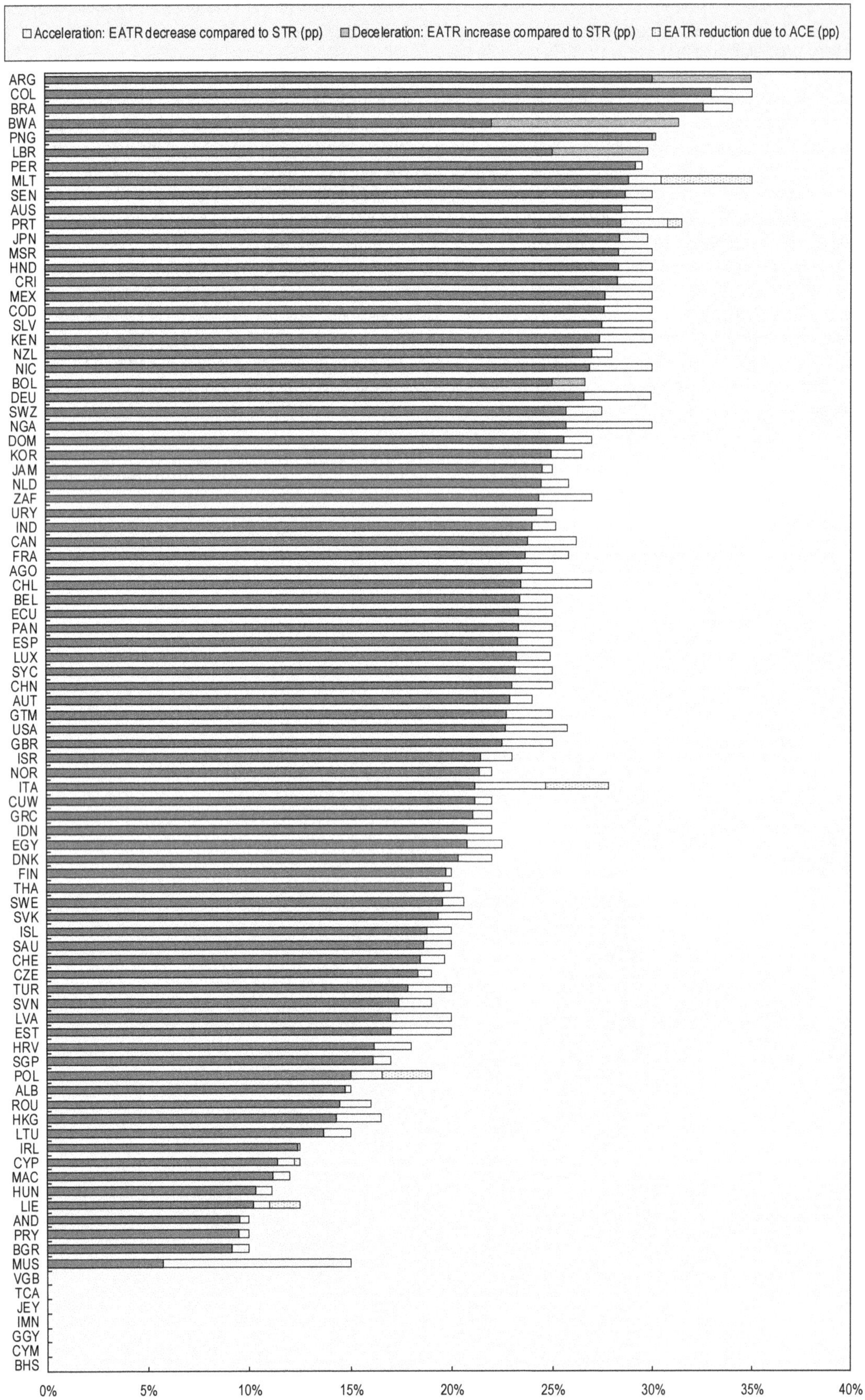

Note: The values of EATRs are calculated assuming a fixed inflation rate at 1% and fixed real interest rate at 3% and setting the pre-tax rate of return from investments at 20%. Additional parameters are outlined in the Effective Tax Rate (ETR) explanatory annex accompanying *Corporate Tax Statistics*. https://www.oecd.org/tax/tax-policy/explanatory-annex-corporate-effective-tax-rates.pdf. Note additional details on the modelling of ETRs for Poland and Saudi Arabia.
Poland: The value of ACE in Poland is capped at PLN 250 000 per tax year. The presence of caps or limitations on the use of ACEs are not captured on the ETR modelling. For taxpayers for which the cap is binding, the impact on ETRs of the ACE would be lower.
Saudi Arabia: The Kingdom of Saudi Arabia imposes a corporate income tax rate of 20% on a non-Saudi's' share of a resident company or a non-resident's income from a permanent establishment in Saudi Arabia or income of a company operating in the natural gas sector. A higher corporate income tax rate is imposed as well on companies operating in the oil sector (i.e., 50% or higher). The Kingdom of Saudi Arabia also levies the Zakat on companies, which is an example of a tax on both income and equity. The Zakat is levied at 2.5% on a Saudi's share of a resident company (also applies to citizens of Gulf Cooperation Council countries with an established business in the Kingdom of Saudi Arabia), but since it is imposed on income and equity, it yields a higher rate in effective terms. The Saudi government considers the corporate Zakat as an equivalent to corporate income tax, levied on a different basis. It is also considered a covered tax for the purposes of the GloBE rules in the Pillar 2 Blueprint Report (OECD, 2020). For the calculation of the forward-looking ETRs, three different groups of taxpayers are considered: (i) foreign companies as well as domestic and foreign companies in the natural gas sector taxed at 20%, (ii) domestic and foreign companies in the hydrocarbon sector taxed at 50%, (iii) other domestic companies taxed through Zakat at 2.5%. The results for these three groups of taxpayers are weighted using the respective turnover shares as weights, i.e., 18.17% for group (i), 28.72% for group (ii) and 53.11% for group (iii). The composite EATR corresponds to the combination of the unshaded and shaded blue components of each bar.
Source: *Corporate Tax Statistics* Effective Tax Rates

StatLink https://stat.link/x39jni

Box 4.1. Key concepts and methodology

Forward-looking effective tax rates (ETRs) are calculated on the basis of a prospective, hypothetical investment project. The OECD methodology has been described in detail in the OECD Taxation Working Paper No. 38 (Hanappi, 2018[1]), building on the theoretical model developed by Devereux and Griffith (1998[2]; 2003[3]). The methodology builds on the following key concepts:

- **Economic profits** are defined as the difference between total revenue and total economic costs, including explicit costs involved in the production of goods and services as well as opportunity costs such as, for example, revenue foregone by using company-owned buildings or self-employment resources. It is calculated as the net present value (NPV) over all cash flows associated with the investment project.
- **The user cost of capital** is defined as the pre-tax rate of return on capital required to generate zero post-tax economic profits. In contrast, the real interest rate is the return on capital earned in the alternative case, for example, if the investment would not be undertaken and the funds would remain in a bank account.
- **The tax-exclusive effective marginal tax rate** measures the extent to which taxation increases the user cost of capital; it corresponds to the case of a marginal project that delivers just enough profit to break even but no economic profit over and above this threshold. The tax exclusive EMTR uses the real interest rate as the denominator to avoid misspecification at negative values of the cost of capital. Which may arise e.g., due to tax incentives. The tax inclusive EMTR instead uses the cost of capital in the denominator.

$$EMTR = \frac{(Cost\ of\ capital) - (Real\ interest\ rate)}{Real\ interest\ rate}$$

- **The effective average tax rate** reflects the average tax contribution a firm makes on an investment project earning above-zero economic profits. It is defined as the difference in pre-tax and post-tax economic profits relative to the NPV of pre-tax income net of real economic depreciation.

$$EATR = \frac{\left(Economic\ profit_{NPV}^{pre-tax}\right) - \left(Economic\ profit_{NPV}^{post-tax}\right)}{\left(Net\ income_{NPV}^{pre-tax}\right)}$$

- **Real economic depreciation** is a measure of the decrease in the productive value of an asset over time; depreciation patterns of a given asset type can be estimated using asset prices in resale markets. The OECD methodology uses economic depreciation estimates from the US Bureau of Economic Analysis (BEA, 2003[4]).
- Jurisdiction-specific tax codes typically provide **capital allowances** to reflect the decrease in asset value over time in the calculation of taxable profits. If capital allowances match the decay of the asset's value resulting from it being used in production, then fiscal depreciation equals economic depreciation.
- If capital allowances are more generous relative to economic depreciation, fiscal depreciation is **accelerated**; where capital allowances are less generous, fiscal depreciation is referred to as **decelerated**. The NPV of capital allowances, measured as percentage of the initial investment, accounts for timing effects on the value of capital allowances, thus providing comparable information on the generosity of fiscal depreciation across assets and jurisdictions.

The cost of capital, EMTR, EATR as well as the NPV of capital allowances are all available for 90 jurisdictions in the *Corporate Tax Statistics* online database.

Box 4.2. Asset categories and tax provisions covered

The calculations build on a comprehensive coverage of jurisdiction-specific tax rules pertaining to four asset categories.

1. **Buildings** including non-residential structure such as, e.g., manufacturing plants, large engineering structures, office or commercial buildings
2. **Tangible assets** including five specific asset groups: road transport vehicles; air, rail or water transport vehicles; computer hardware; equipment and industrial machinery
3. **Inventories** including, e.g., goods or raw materials in stock
4. **Acquired software** such as computer programmes or applications that a company acquires for commercial purposes

For this edition of *Corporate Tax Statistics*, the data collection process for the tangible asset category has been disaggregated to further improve the cross-country comparability of the ETR data series. Since tangible assets are a particularly broad asset category, collecting disaggregated information on asset-specific tax rules ensures that the variation across specific assets is better captured within this category.

The following corporate tax provisions are covered:

- combined central and sub-central CIT rates;
- asset-specific fiscal depreciation rules, including first-year allowances, half-year or mid-month conventions;
- general tax incentives only if available for a broad group of investments undertaken by large domestic or multinational firms;
- inventory valuation methods including first-in-first-out last-in-first-out and average cost methods;
- allowances for corporate equity.

The composite ETRs reported in this publication are constructed in three steps. First, ETRs are calculated separately for each jurisdiction, asset category and source of finance (debt and equity); within the tangible asset category, ETRs are first calculated separately for each of the five disaggregated assets and then combined through an unweighted average. While the debt-finance case accounts for interest deductibility, jurisdiction-specific limitations to interest deductibility have not been covered in this edition. Second, an unweighted average over the asset categories is taken, separately for both sources of finance. Third, the composite ETRs are obtained as a weighted average between equity- and debt-financed investments, applying a weight of 65% equity and 35% debt finance.

Box 4.3. Macroeconomic scenarios

The two main macroeconomic parameters used in the models, inflation and interest rates, interact with the effects of the tax system in various ways and can have significant effects on ETRs.

The *Corporate Tax Statistics* database contains ETR results for two different macroeconomic scenarios. In the first scenario, interest and inflation rates are held constant; the second scenario uses jurisdiction-specific macroeconomic parameters. While the former approach addresses the question of how differences in tax systems compare across jurisdictions holding other factors constant, the latter approach gives some indications about the effects of varying macroeconomic conditions on investment incentives as captured by the ETRs.

The results published in this publication build exclusively on the macroeconomic scenario with constant 3% interest and 1% inflation rates, however, results from the other macroeconomic scenario are available in the online database.

Figure 4.2. Changing distribution of corporate effective average tax rates, 2017-2023

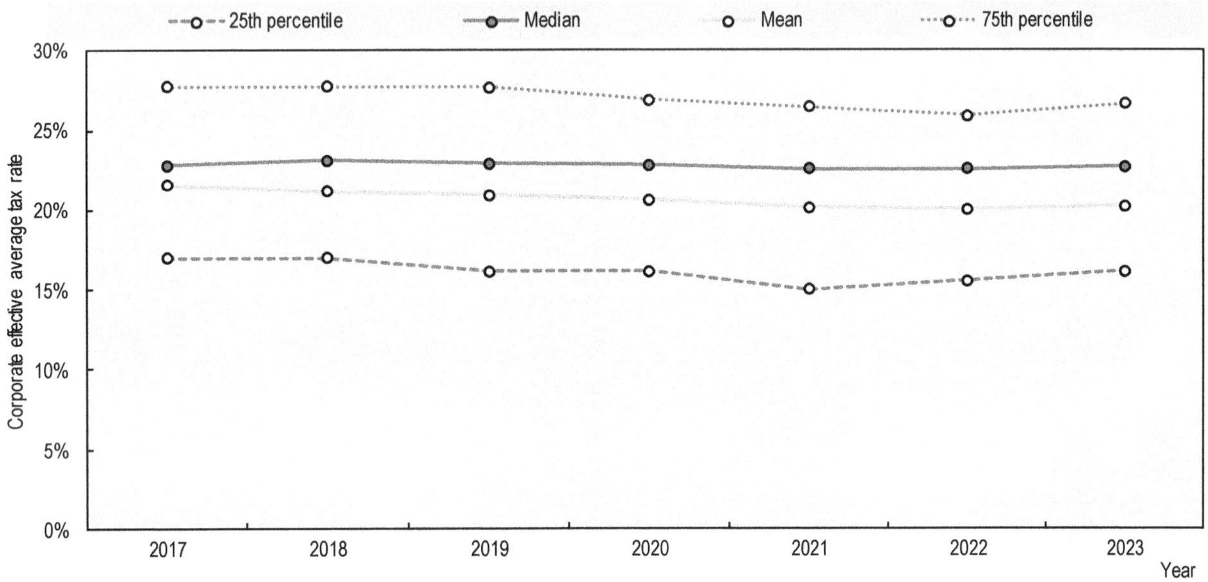

Note: The values of EATRs are calculated assuming a fixed inflation rate at 1% and fixed real interest rate at 3% and setting the pre-tax rate of return from investments at 20%. Additional parameters are outlined in the ETR explanatory annex accompanying *Corporate Tax Statistics*. https://www.oecd.org/tax/tax-policy/explanatory-annex-corporate-effective-tax-rates.pdf.

StatLink https://stat.link/9lrza7

Effective marginal tax rates

Figure 4.3 shows the ranking based on the composite EMTR. As highlighted above, the EMTR measures the effects of taxation on the pre-tax rate of return required by investors to break even. While the effects of tax depreciation and macroeconomic parameters work in the same direction as in the case of the EATR, their impacts on the EMTR will generally be stronger because marginal projects do not earn economic profits (see Box 4.1). As a consequence, jurisdictions with relatively high statutory CIT rates and relatively generous capital allowances, notably Italy the United Kingdom and the United States, rank lower than in Figure 4.1. On the other hand, jurisdictions with less generous fiscal depreciation rules, including Argentina, Japan, New Zealand, Papua New Guinea and Peru (as well as Botswana, Liberia, and Czechia), are ranked higher based on the EMTR, as shown in Figure 4.3.

Figure 4.3. Effective marginal tax rate, 2023

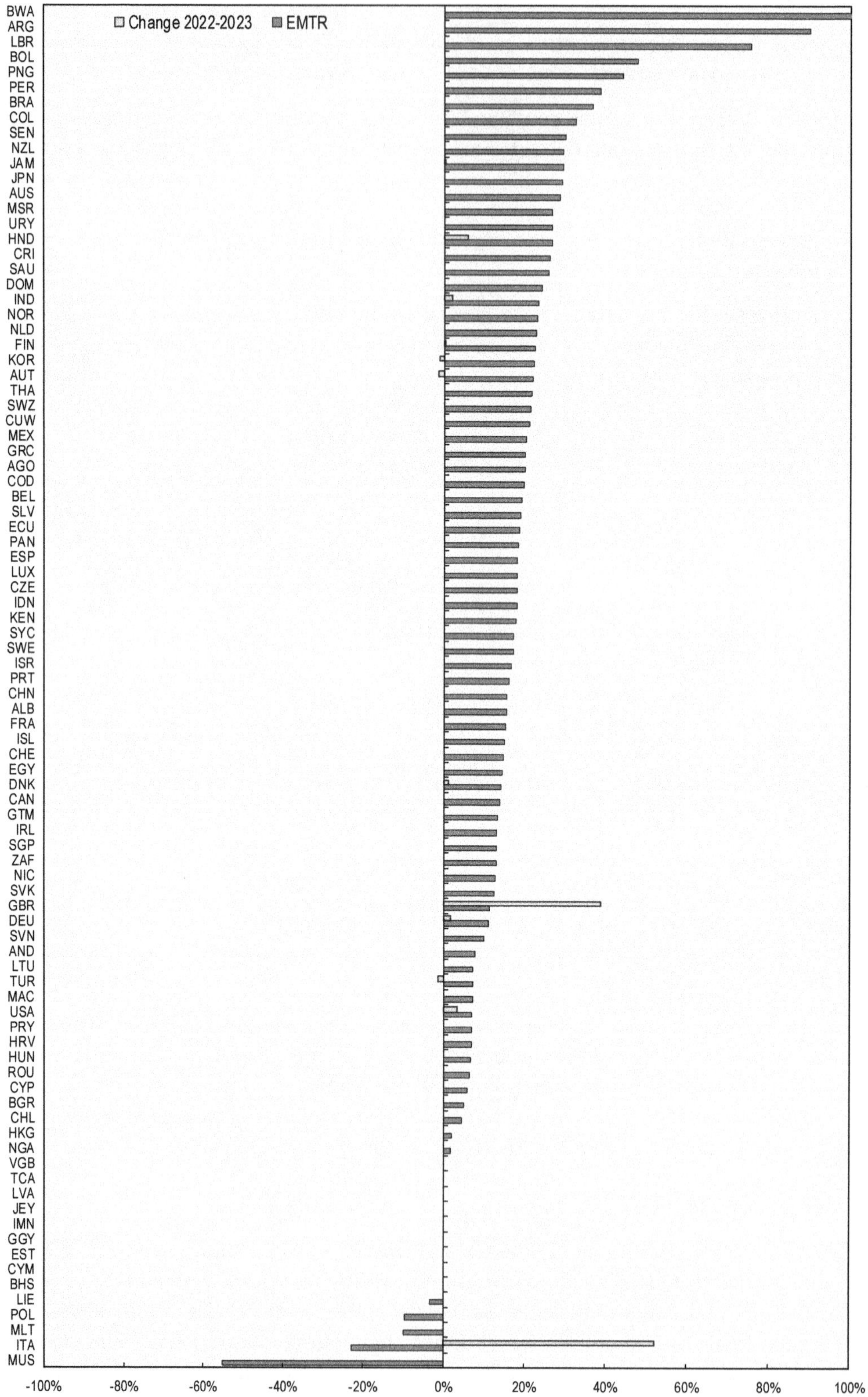

Note: The values of EMTRs are calculated assuming a fixed inflation rate at 1% and fixed real interest rate at 3% and setting the pre-tax rate of return from investments at 20%. The EMTR is computed using the tax exclusive definition (Box 4.1). Additional parameters are outlined in the ETR explanatory annex accompanying *Corporate Tax Statistics*. https://oe.cd/5hb.

StatLink https://stat.link/yjesub

Where investment projects are financed by debt, it is also possible for the EMTR to be negative, which means that the tax system, notably through interest deductibility, reduces the pre-tax rate of return required to break even and thus enables projects that would otherwise not have been economically viable. Figure 4.3 shows that the composite EMTR, based on a weighted average between equity- and debt-financed projects, is negative in 5 out of 90 jurisdictions; this result is due to the combination of debt finance with comparatively generous tax depreciation rules. For jurisdictions with an ACE, the composite EMTR will generally be lower because of the notional interest deduction available for equity-financed projects.

Comparing EMTRs in 2023 with the previous year shows that changes in the corporate tax provisions covered in the calculations had significant effects on EMTRs in several countries. On the one hand, 9 jurisdictions have decreased the generosity of their tax depreciation rules, resulting in an increase in the EMTRs in 2023 compared to 2022; this group includes the United Kingdom (38 p.p.) among others. On the other hand, three jurisdictions have increased the generosity of their tax depreciation rules, leading to lower EMTRs in 2023 than in 2022; this group includes Austria, Türkiye (both 1.3 p.p.), and Korea (1.2 p.p.).

Figure 4.4. Changing distribution of corporate effective marginal tax rates, 2017-2023

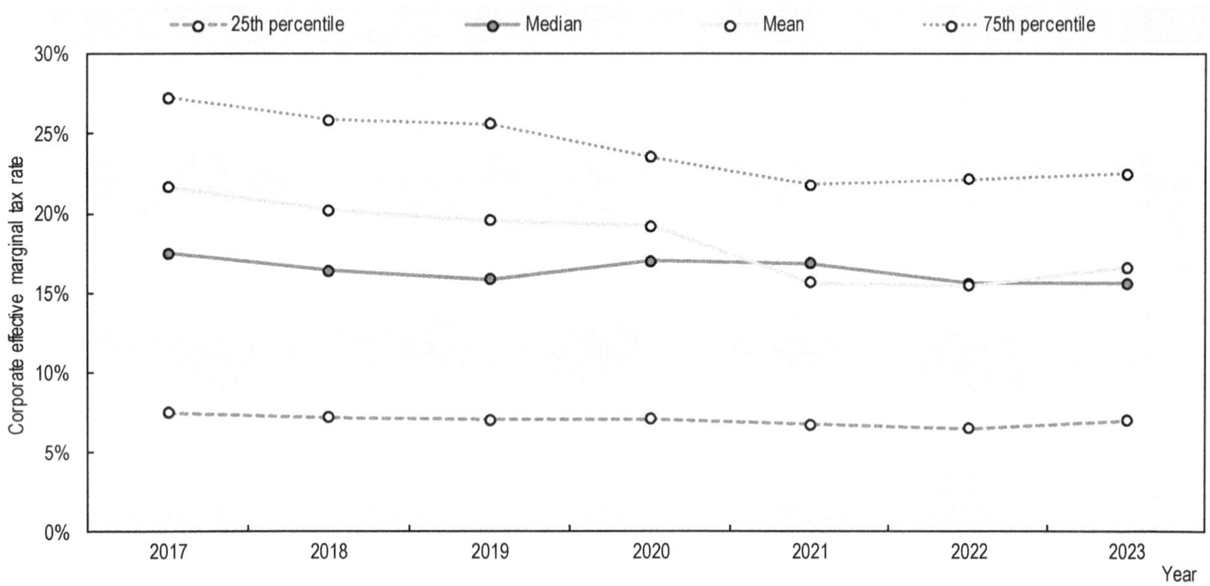

Note: The values of EMTRs are calculated assuming a fixed inflation rate at 1% and fixed real interest rate at 3% and setting the pre-tax rate of return from investments at 20%. The EMTR is computed using the tax exclusive definition (Box 4.1). Additional parameters are outlined in the ETR explanatory annex accompanying *Corporate Tax Statistics*. https://www.oecd.org/tax/tax-policy/explanatory-annex-corporate-effective-tax-rates.pdf.

StatLink https://stat.link/7smjp8

The distribution of EMTRs saw a general downward trend between 2017-2023 throughout the distribution. The median EMTR has dropped from 17.5% in 2017 to 15.6% in 2023, while at the top and bottom of the distribution the 75th and 25th percentile dropped from 27.3% and 7.5% respectively in 2017 to 22.5% and 6.9% in 2023. The average EMTRs have fallen from 21.6% in 2017 to 16.6% in 2023, although there was an increase from 15.4% in 2022. This latter increase is mainly due to increases in the EMTR for Italy and the United Kingdom.

Effective tax rates by asset categories

The composite ETRs can be further disaggregated by asset categories; jurisdiction-level EATRs and EMTRs by asset categories are available in the online *Corporate Tax Statistics* database. Figure 4.5 summarises these data on ETRs by asset category. The upper panel provides more information on the distribution of asset specific EATRs, comparing them to the distribution of statutory CIT rates. The first vertical line depicts information on the statutory CIT rates; it shows that the mean (i.e., the circle in the middle of the first vertical line) and the median (the light blue triangle) are around 21.2% and 25% respectively, while the 50% of jurisdictions in the middle of the distribution have statutory CIT rates between 16.9% and 27.6%.

The other four vertical lines in the upper panel of Figure 4.5 illustrate the distribution of EATRs across jurisdictions for each of the four asset categories: buildings, tangible assets, inventories and acquired software. Since there is more variation in economic and tax-related characteristics across tangible assets, this category summarises information on investments in several specific tangible assets, i.e., air, railroad and water transport vehicles, road transport vehicles, computer hardware, industrial machinery and equipment (see Box 4.2).

Figure 4.5. EATR and EMTR: Variation across jurisdictions and assets, 2023

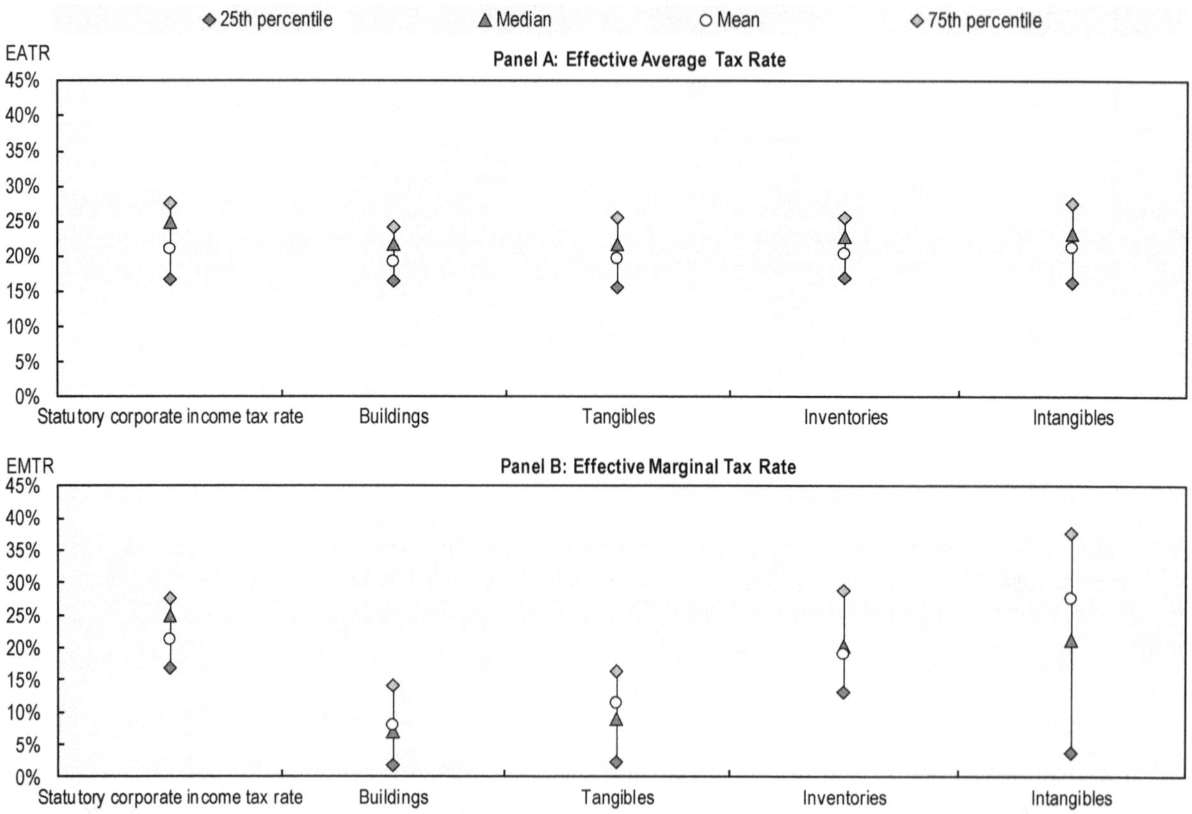

Note: The values of EMTRs and EATRs are calculated assuming a fixed inflation rate at 1% and fixed real interest rate at 3% and setting the pre-tax rate of return from investments at 20%. The EMTR is computed using the tax exclusive definition (Box 4.1). Additional parameters are outlined in the ETR explanatory annex accompanying *Corporate Tax Statistics*. https://www.oecd.org/tax/tax-policy/explanatory-annex-corporate-effective-tax-rates.pdf.

StatLink https://stat.link/e0lzfx

Comparing the four broader asset categories with the statutory CIT rate shows that the distribution of EATRs is more condensed for investments in buildings, with the middle 50% of the country distribution ranging between 16.6% and 24.2%. For investments in tangible assets, the middle 50% of jurisdictions have EATRs between around 15.6% and 25.5%. However, the mean EATR (19.7%) on investments in tangible assets is around 2.1 p.p. lower than the median (21.8%), indicating that some jurisdictions have much lower EATRs on this type of investment. For investments in the other two asset categories, the distributions are similar to the statutory tax rate.

The lower panel illustrates the EMTR distribution for each of the four broader asset categories. The following insights emerge from this graph.

- Investments in buildings and tangible assets benefit more often from accelerated tax depreciation than other investments; as a result, the EMTRs are generally lower.
- Investments in buildings have EMTRs ranging between 1.8% and 14.0% in half of the covered jurisdictions.
- Investments in inventories often benefit from lower EMTRs, compared to the statutory tax rate, although to a lesser extent than the first two asset categories.
- The tax treatment of investments in acquired software is subject to more variation across jurisdictions, which is reflected in the vertical line that stretches out more than the others, ranging from around 3.9% to around 37.7%.

Figure 4.6. Changing distribution of EATRs by assets, 2017-2023

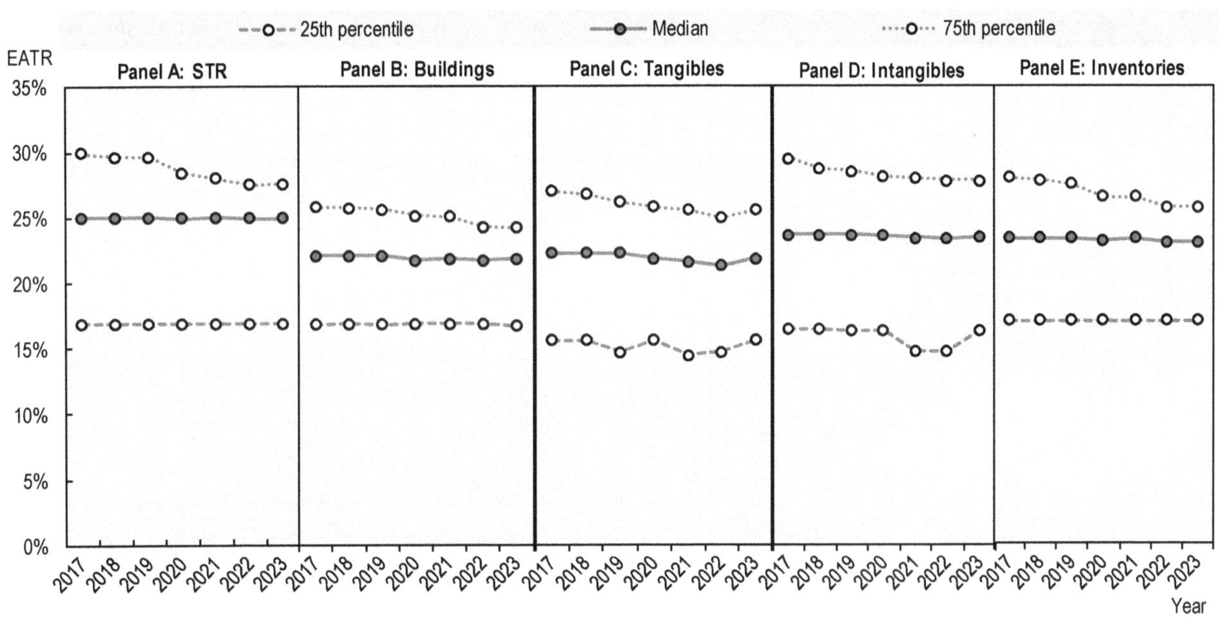

Note: The values of the EATRs are calculated assuming a fixed inflation rate at 1% and fixed real interest rate at 3% and setting the pre-tax rate of return from investments at 20%. Additional parameters are outlined in the ETR explanatory annex accompanying *Corporate Tax Statistics*. https://www.oecd.org/tax/tax-policy/explanatory-annex-corporate-effective-tax-rates.pdf.

StatLink https://stat.link/2f57yz

When comparing Figure 4.2 to Figure 4.6, it appears that the downward trend in EATRs between 2017 and 2023 did not occur consistently throughout all asset groups and their respective distributions. While the composite EATR shows an overall decline in the 25th percentile between 2017 and 2023, the 25th percentile of the EATRs for buildings and inventories (Panels B and E) remained relatively stable during those years. During the same period the 25th percentile for tangibles and intangibles were more volatile in comparison. Between 2017 and 2023, the 75th percentile of the EATR distribution has decreased consistently for inventories and intangibles while 2023 has seen an increase in the 75th percentile for tangibles. By contrast, between 2020 and 2021 the drop in EATRs for intangibles was stronger in jurisdictions at the lower end of the distribution. With the exception of the 25th percentiles for tangibles and intangibles the evolution of the values for each group follow that of the STR closely.

Comparing median EMTRs over time, tangible assets and buildings face significantly lower EMTRs than the other asset categories. Figure 4.7 shows the distribution of the EMTRs disaggregated by asset types and over time. The dispersion of EMTRs is particularly marked for acquired intangibles (Panel D). This reflects important differences in the fiscal depreciation provisions applicable to acquired software between jurisdictions. Several jurisdictions in the database offer very stringent depreciation rules for acquired software. In some cases, it is non depreciable, which drives the EMTR of this asset category above the STR. Notably, the dispersion of EMTRs for tangible assets has tended to decrease over time, notably for countries at the top of the distribution.

Figure 4.7. Changing distribution of EMTRs by assets, 2017-2023

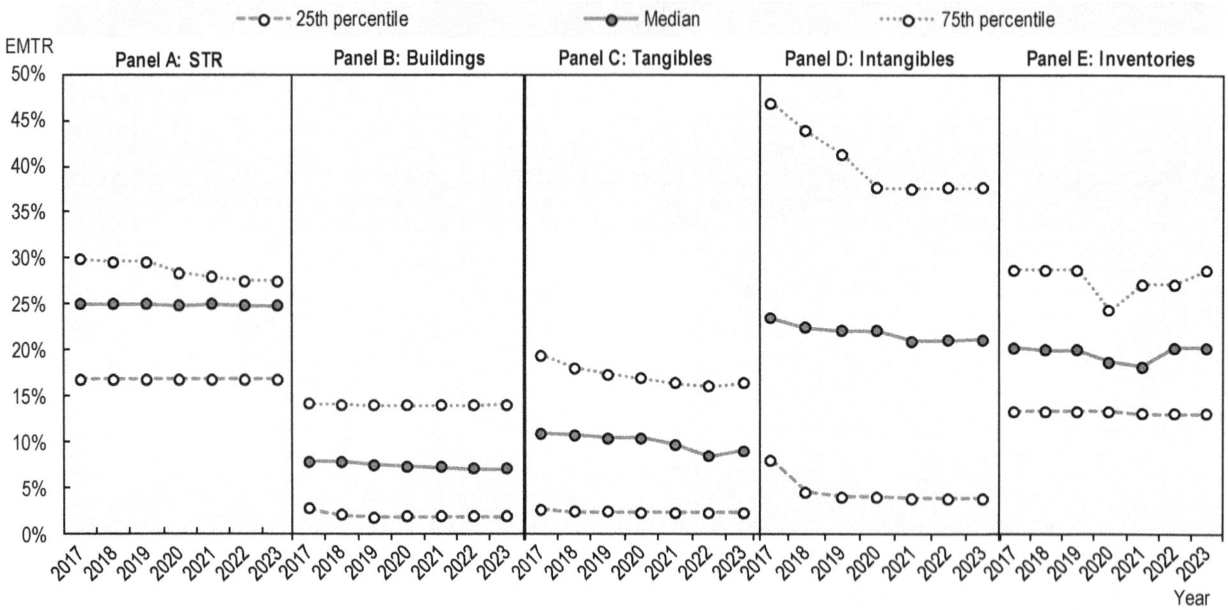

Note: The values of EMTRs are calculated assuming a fixed inflation rate at 1% and fixed real interest rate at 3% and setting the pre-tax rate of return from investments at 20%. The EMTR is computed using the tax exclusive definition (Box 4.1). Additional parameters are outlined in the ETR explanatory annex accompanying *Corporate Tax Statistics*. https://www.oecd.org/tax/tax-policy/explanatory-annex-corporate-effective-tax-rates.pdf.

StatLink https://stat.link/wl14m9

When comparing the distribution of disaggregated EMTRs with that of EATRs, the former - as depicted by Figure 4.7 - exhibits more heterogeneity both within and between asset categories. The figure shows that during the years of coverage, the EMTR applicable to investments in buildings and tangible assets as well as the EMTR applicable to inventories are consistently lower than the STR. The median EMTR for buildings and tangible assets is lower than 10% throughout the period 2017-2023 while the median STR remains around 25%. This contrast reflects that baseline CIT systems tend to provide generous fiscal depreciation for these asset types, thereby significantly reducing the cost of capital (a key element in the derivation of the EMTR) and reducing the effective tax burden on investments at the intensive margin.

Changes in the distribution of EMTR by asset type highlight the effects of certain tax reforms. Whereas Figure 4.4 shows a large drop in the average EMTR between 2020 and 2021, the equivalent disaggregated figure informs that this drop was neither consistent between asset groups nor within the respective distributions of asset groups. Panel C shows that an important part of the drop was driven by the relief in tax burden for marginal investments in tangible assets – particularly for jurisdictions at the top end of the distribution such as Italy and the United Kingdom where the EMTR for tangible assets dropped by 5.0 and 4.2 p.p., respectively. During those two years, the 75th and 25th percentiles as well as the median for EMTRs applicable to buildings remained about constant. By contrast, the median values for intangibles and inventories both decreased during the same period.

References

BEA (2003), *Fixed Assets and Consumer Durable Goods in the United States, 1925-97 | U.S. Bureau of Economic Analysis (BEA)*, https://www.bea.gov/node/24441 (accessed on 18 February 2023). [4]

Devereux, M. and R. Griffith (2003), "Evaluating tax policy for location decisions", *International Tax and Public Finance*, Vol. 10/2, pp. 107-126, https://doi.org/10.1023/A:1023364421914. [3]

Devereux, M. and R. Griffith (1998), "The taxation of discrete investment choices", https://www.econstor.eu/handle/10419/90851 (accessed on 18 February 2023). [2]

Hanappi, T. (2018), "Corporate Effective Tax Rates: Model Description and Results from 36 OECD and Non-OECD Countries", *OECD Taxation Working Papers*, No. 38, OECD Publishing, Paris, https://doi.org/10.1787/a07f9958-en. [1]

5 Tax incentives for research and development

Key insights

- Both income and expenditure-based tax incentives for research and development (R&D) are increasingly used to promote business R&D. Expenditure-based incentives are widely used; with 33 out of the 38 OECD jurisdictions offering tax relief on R&D expenditures in 2023, compared to 19 in 2000. Income-based incentives are slightly less widely offered; with 21 OECD countries providing these incentives, an increase from 4 in 2000.
- Most jurisdictions use a combination of direct support and tax relief to support business R&D, but the policy mix varies. Over time, there has been a shift towards a more intensive use of expenditure-based R&D tax incentives to deliver financial support for business R&D. Income-based incentives are often used together with expenditure-based incentives. With the exception of Luxembourg, every country with an income-based incentive also has an expenditure-based incentive.
- The effective average tax rate (EATR) for R&D incorporating expenditure-based tax incentives in 2023 was lowest in Ireland, Poland and Lithuania, providing greater tax incentives for firms to locate R&D investment in these jurisdictions. The average across the 48 jurisdictions covered in the baseline scenario was 14.2%, or 7.1 percentage points below the standard tax treatment.
- The cost of capital for R&D in 2023 incorporating expenditure-based tax incentives was lowest in Portugal, Poland and France where these jurisdictions provide greater tax incentives for firms to increase their R&D investment. The average across the 48 jurisdictions covered in the baseline scenario was 0.3%, or 2.8 percentage points below the standard tax treatment.
- For profitable small and medium-sized enterprises (SMEs), implied marginal R&D tax subsidy rates were highest in Colombia, Iceland and Portugal in 2022.
- The effective average tax rate (EATR) for R&D incorporating income-based tax incentives in 2023 was lowest in Malta. The average across the 48 jurisdictions covered in the baseline scenario was 12.7%, or 6.8 percentage points below the standard tax treatment.
- The cost of capital for R&D in 2023 incorporating income-based tax incentives was lowest in Israel. The average across the 48 jurisdictions covered in the baseline scenario was 3.9%, or 0.25 percentage points below the standard tax treatment.
- While the income-based and expenditure-based models are not directly comparable, these indicators highlight that expenditure-based incentives provide a relatively greater impact on the cost of capital compared to income-based incentives.
- R&D tax incentives have become more generous, on average, over time. This is due to the higher uptake and increased generosity of R&D tax relief provisions. While this trend stabilised between 2013 and 2019, an increase in generosity is again observed from 2020 and maintained through to 2022. The generosity of income-based incentives has increased over time, but has remained more stable since 2019.

Incentivising investment in R&D by businesses ranks high on the innovation policy agenda of many jurisdictions. R&D tax incentives have become a widely used policy tool to promote business R&D over recent decades. Several jurisdictions offer them in addition to direct forms of support such as R&D grants or government purchases of R&D services. R&D tax incentives can provide relief to R&D expenditures, such as the wages of R&D staff and/or to the income derived from R&D activities, such as patent income. This chapter covers both indicators referred to in this section relate to expenditure-based R&D tax incentives and income-based R&D tax incentives to R&D and innovation. Further information on income-based tax incentives is available in the section on Intellectual Property (IP) regimes. In this section, income-based tax incentives cover IP regimes which apply only to IP income as well as regimes that also extend support to other forms of non-IP income (dual category regimes). The significant variation in the design of expenditure-based R&D tax relief provisions across jurisdictions and over time affects the implied generosity of R&D tax incentives.

Indicators of R&D tax incentives

The *Corporate Tax Statistics* database incorporates two sets of R&D tax incentives indicators that offer a complementary view of the extent of R&D tax support provided through expenditure-based R&D tax incentives. A third set of indicators focus on income-based R&D tax incentives.

The first set of indicators reflects the cost of expenditure-based tax incentives to the government:

- Government tax relief for business R&D (GTARD) includes estimates of foregone revenue (and refundable amounts) from national and subnational incentives, where applicable and relevant data are available. This indicator is complemented with figures on direct funding of business R&D to provide a more complete picture of total government support to business R&D investment.
- Both indicators, compiled by the OECD Directorate for Science, Technology and Innovation, are available for 48 jurisdictions – OECD jurisdictions and 10 partner economies – for the period 2000-2021.

The second set of indicators are synthetic tax policy indicators that capture the effect of expenditure-based R&D tax incentives on firms' investment costs (see Box 5.1):

- The EATR for R&D measures the impact of taxation on R&D investments that earn an economic profit.
- The user cost of capital for R&D measures the return that a firm needs to realise on an R&D investment before tax to offset all costs and taxes that arise from the investment, making zero economic profit.
- Implied marginal tax subsidy rates for R&D, calculated as 1 minus the B-Index, reflect the design and implied generosity of R&D tax incentives to firms for an extra unit of R&D outlay. The B-Index captures the extent to which different tax systems reduce the effective cost of R&D.

The third set of indicators are also synthetic tax policy indicators, but capturing the effect of income-based R&D tax incentives on firms' investment costs.

- As for expenditure-based tax incentives, EATRs, the user cost of capital, and the B-index are calculated for income-based tax incentives.

The second and third set of indicators are available for 48 countries, including OECD jurisdictions and ten partner economies. Indicators of the user cost of capital and the EATR for expenditure-based incentives are available for 2019-2022, while for income-based they are available from 2000-2022. All indicators refer to large businesses who are able to fully utilise their tax benefits. Indicators of the large companies account for the bulk of the R&D in most OECD countries (OECD, 2022a[1]; Dernis et al., 2019[2]). The EATR and user cost for R&D are produced by the OECD Centre for Tax Policy and Administration and the OECD Directorate for Science, Technology and Innovation. The B-Index for expenditure-based incentives, which is, compiled by the OECD Directorate for Science, Technology and Innovation, covers a wider group of firm scenarios (SMEs; large firms; profit and loss-making) over the 2000-2022 time period.

The indicators of ETRs and cost of capital for R&D in this section chapter extend the corporate ETRs shown in the previous chapter section to include internally generated R&D assets, i.e., those that are the result of a firms' own R&D.[1]

Expenditure-based tax incentives

Government support for business R&D

Indicators of government tax relief for business R&D combined with data on direct R&D funding provide a more complete picture of governments' efforts to support business expenditure on R&D (BERD). Together, these indicators facilitate the cross-jurisdiction comparison of the policy mix provided by governments to support R&D and the monitoring of any changes over time.

Figure 5.1. Direct government funding and expenditure-based tax support for business R&D (BERD), 2021

As a percentage of gross domestic product (GDP)

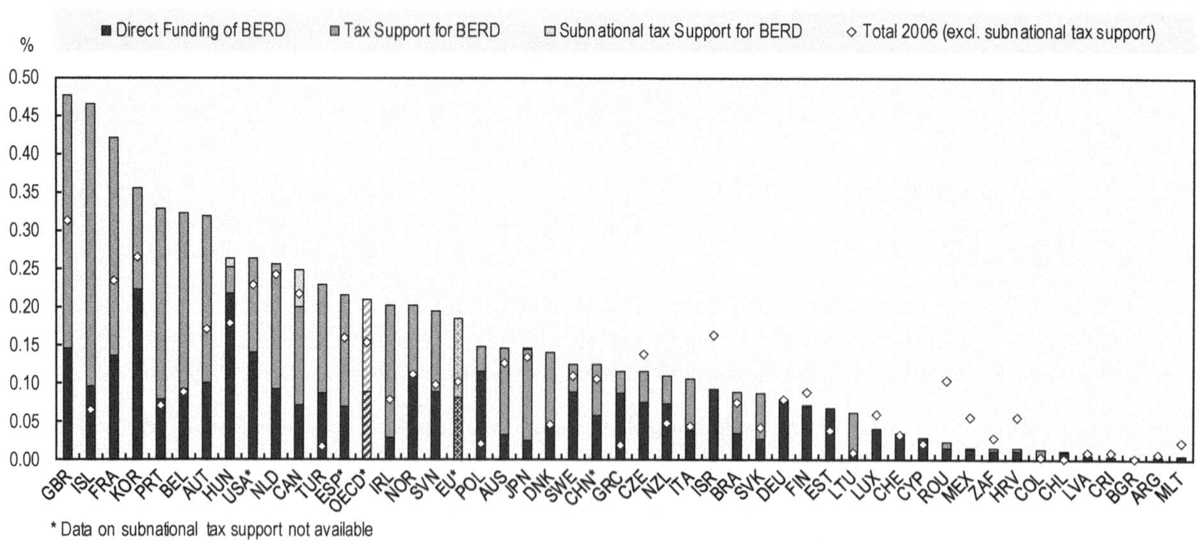

Data and notes: https://oe.cd/rdtax. Time series data available for 2000-2021.
Source: OECD (2023), R&D Tax Incentive Database, http://oe.cd/rdtax, April 2024, (accessed in May 2024).

StatLink https://stat.link/7tcdam

Between 2006 and 2021, total government support (direct and national tax support) for business R&D expenditure as a percentage of GDP increased in 33 out of 48 jurisdictions for which relevant data are available. The United Kingdom, Iceland and France provided the largest levels of support in 2021 (Figure 5.1). Subnational R&D tax incentives accounted for 25% of total tax support in Canada in 2021, playing a comparatively smaller role in Hungary and Japan (nearly 5% and 1% of total tax support, respectively).

Most jurisdictions integrate both direct and indirect forms of R&D support in their policy mix, but to different degrees. In 2021, 19 OECD jurisdictions offered more than 50% of government support for business R&D through the tax system, and this percentage reached 75% or more in seven OECD jurisdictions: Australia, Colombia, Ireland, Iceland, Japan, Lithuania and Portugal. Eight OECD jurisdictions relied solely on direct support in 2021. These are Costa Rica, Estonia, Finland, Germany, Israel, Latvia, Luxembourg and Switzerland.

Combining time-series estimates of GTARD and direct funding helps illustrate variations in governments' policy mix over time. In recent years, many jurisdictions have granted a more prominent role to R&D tax incentives. Compared to 2006, the share of tax support in total government support in 2021 increased in 29 out of 38 OECD jurisdictions for which data are available. This implies a general shift towards less discretionary forms of support for business R&D, with some exceptions, e.g., Canada and Hungary increased their reliance on direct support.

Measuring the preferential tax treatment for R&D

R&D tax incentives exhibit very heterogeneous design features across jurisdictions, which come on top of existing differences in standard corporate income tax systems. Indicators based on forward-looking effective tax rates are therefore useful to capture the effect of taxation on firms' R&D in a synthetic manner investment incentives. By fixing the composition of the R&D investment, they enable comparisons of the preferential tax treatment provided for R&D investments across jurisdictions.

This database provides a toolbox for policymakers to analyse the incentives that firms face through the tax system to increase their R&D investment in a given country or to (re)locate their R&D functions, taking into account both the impact of underlying corporate taxation as well as specific R&D tax incentives. Indicators calculating the EATR and the cost of capital for R&D are useful to analyse decisions at the extensive margin (e.g., whether or where to invest in R&D) and at the intensive margin (e.g., how much to invest in R&D), respectively. These indicators focus on the incentives faced by large firms among which R&D is heavily concentrated (OECD, 2022a[1]; Dernis et al., 2019[2]) and assume that firms are able to use their tax benefits in full.

Governments often introduce specific provisions to target particular firm types and to promote R&D among firms that may not be able to fully use their tax benefits. The B-Index, tightly related to the cost of capital, is another useful indicator to analyse R&D investment decisions at the intensive margin and to compare differences in the implied R&D tax subsidy rates among different firm types (SMEs and large firms) and profit scenarios (profit and loss). Box 5.1 provides an overview of the three indicators.

Box 5.1. Three complementary indicators of the generosity of R&D tax support

The cost of capital, the B-Index and the EATR are conceptually linked and rely on the same modelling of R&D tax incentives. As indicators of the cost of R&D for a marginal unit of R&D outlay, the B-Index and cost of capital are used in the economic literature to assess firms' R&D investment decisions at the intensive margin, e.g., how much to invest in R&D.

The **B-Index** offers a way of comparing the generosity of R&D tax incentives in reducing the upfront investment cost of an R&D investment while abstracting from the financing of the investment. By focussing on the tax component of the cost of capital, the B-index does not require assumptions on the depreciation rate of R&D, which is typically difficult to measure, and directly displays the variation in the tax treatment induced by R&D tax incentives.

The **cost of capital** complements and extends the B-Index indicator by accounting for additional costs and taxes relevant to the R&D investment. Since the cost of capital can in principle account for a variation in economic depreciation across assets and financing options, it also facilitates the analysis of different types of R&D projects. Finally, the cost of capital is also a stepping-stone in the calculation of the EATR.

The **EATR** complements previous indicators by capturing the effect of taxation on profitable investments. This makes the EATR the relevant indicator to assess of investment decisions at the extensive margin (where or whether to invest in R&D). Together, the three indicators offer a complementary set of indicators to assess the impact of taxation on firms' R&D investment decisions.

Source: González Cabral, Appelt and Hanappi. (2021[3])

Incentives at the extensive margin

Comparing the EATRs for R&D investments across jurisdictions gives insights into the expenditure-based incentives provided by the tax system for the location of profitable R&D investments (Figure 5.2, Panel A). The lowest EATRs for R&D investments carried out by large firms are observed in Ireland, Poland and Lithuania, while the highest EATRs for R&D are observed in Argentina, Costa Rica and Colombia. Estimates of the EATR are typically lower for jurisdictions with lower STRs or more generous provisions affecting the tax base, including both standard tax provisions and those specific to R&D investments.

To assess the preferential tax treatment for R&D investments in relation to other investments, it is useful to calculate the EATR for a comparable investment to which expenditure-based R&D tax incentives do not apply. Where available, expenditure-based R&D tax incentives decrease the effective cost of R&D and reduce firms' EATRs, as shown in Panel A by the fact that the diamonds lie lower than the circles. The extent of the reduction, shown in Figure 5.2 Panel B, is explained by the generosity of the expenditure-based R&D tax incentives in each jurisdiction, which is closely linked to the design of these provisions. This figure includes only the impact of tax provisions in supporting R&D: modest reductions, as in Sweden or the United States, may reflect a higher reliance on direct forms of government support for R&D.

By taking the difference between the two EATRs, it is possible to gauge the preferential expenditure-based tax treatment offered to R&D in a given jurisdiction, in isolation from baseline tax provisions available to all types of investments. From a within country perspective, the preferential tax treatment for R&D investments is greatest in France followed, by Poland and Portugal. The absence of bars, as in Costa Rica or Luxembourg, indicates that no preferential expenditure-based tax treatment for R&D is available in the jurisdiction relative to other investment types.

Figure 5.2. The effective average tax rate for R&D including expenditure-based tax incentives, 2023

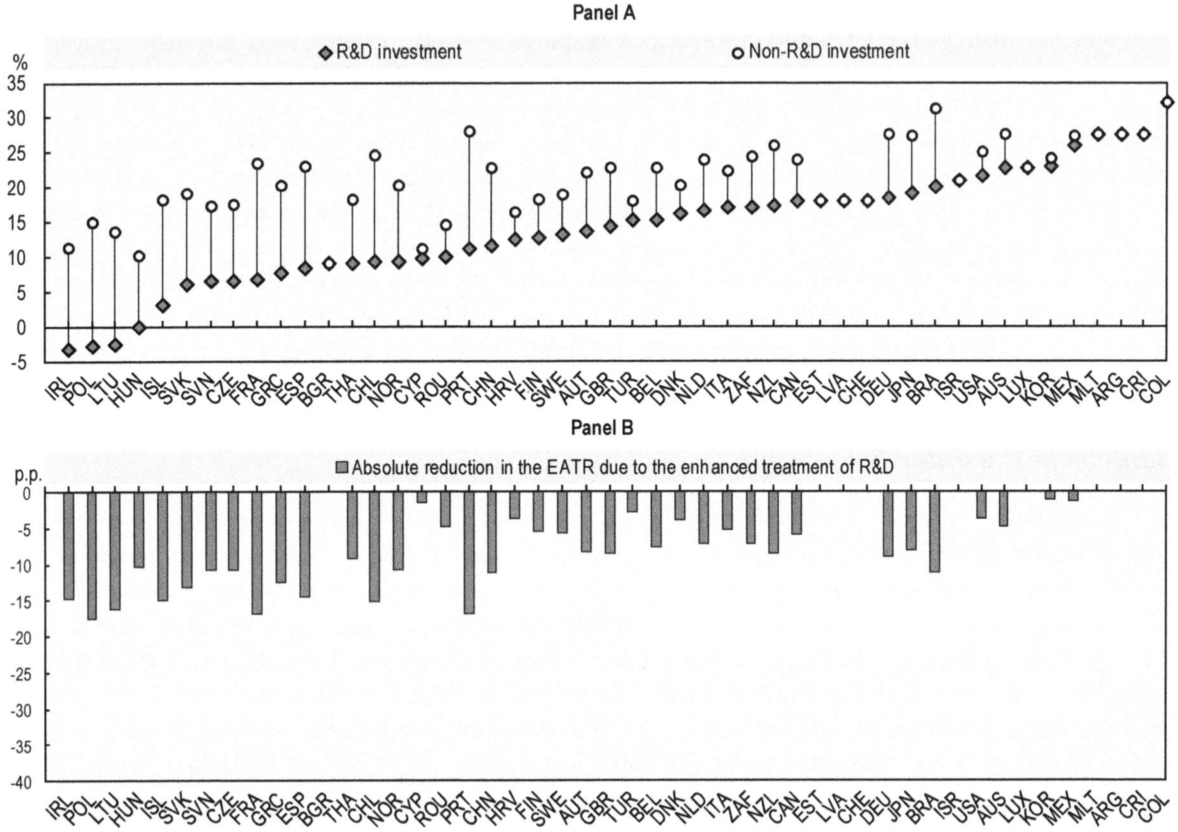

Note: Results refer to a macroeconomic scenario 3% real interest rate and 1% inflation and refer to an investment financed by retained earnings including the effect of allowances for corporate equity where available. In the non-R&D case, the EATRs lie close to the statutory tax rate (STR) due to the large current component in the R&D investment (see Box 5.1), except when an allowance for corporate equity is available.

StatLink https://stat.link/4vxni7

Figure 5.3. Changing distribution of the average EATR for R&D, 2019-2023

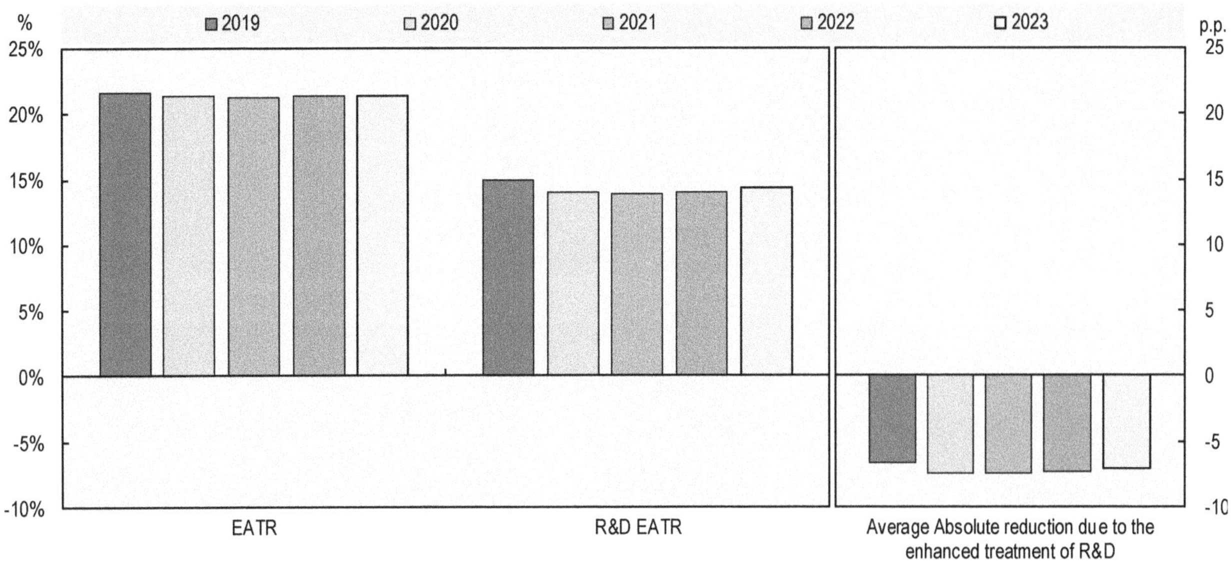

StatLink https://stat.link/2t9cyn

The EATR for R&D including expenditure-based tax incentives has modestly declined over time and while preferential tax treatment has increased compared to 2019, recent years show signs of stabilisation and even small declines in recent years. Figure 5.3 displays average changes to the EATR over time. Consistent with the trends outlined in the baseline effective tax rate (ETR) (Chapter 4), the EATR in the absence of R&D tax incentives have tended to modestly decline over the period covered. A similar but more substantial trend is observable for the EATR once expenditure-based R&D tax incentives are included. The EATR for R&D declined from an average of 14.9% in 2019 to 13.9% in 2020 increasing slightly to 14.2% in 2023. Changes over time in the EATR for R&D are due to first time introductions of expenditure-based incentives (Germany and Denmark in 2020, Finland 2021 or Cyprus in 2022) or changes to the generosity of R&D tax incentives (the Slovak Republic in 2020 and 2022, Italy in 2021 or Poland in 2022). In 2023, expenditure-based R&D tax incentives reduce the average EATR by 33.4%, from 21.3% to 14.2%. Over time, preferential tax treatment has increased between 2019 and 2020 and remained relatively stable between 2020 and 2023.

Incentives at the intensive margin

Once established in a given location, firms decide upon the level of investment with reference to tax provisions that affect the intensive margin. The cost of capital for R&D is one relevant indicator of tax incentives at the intensive margin (see Figure 5.4). Across the jurisdictions considered Portugal, Poland and France are the jurisdictions providing greater incentives through the tax system to increase the volume of R&D. Among jurisdictions offering R&D tax support, estimates of the cost of capital for R&D are highest in Argentina, Costa Rica and Colombia. Estimates of the cost of capital for R&D capture both the variability in standard tax provisions and those specific to R&D investments. R&D tax incentives reduce the cost of capital, with the extent of the reduction being affected by the generosity of R&D tax incentives. The absolute difference between the cost of capital for an R&D investment and a comparable non-R&D investment provides a within-country indication of the magnitude of R&D tax relief to marginal R&D investments, net of the standard tax treatment available to all investments. This allows the preferential tax treatment for R&D to be isolated. The largest reductions in the cost of capital for R&D investments are observed in Poland, Portugal and France, which are among the jurisdictions with the lowest cost of capital estimates.

Figure 5.4. The cost of capital for R&D, 2023

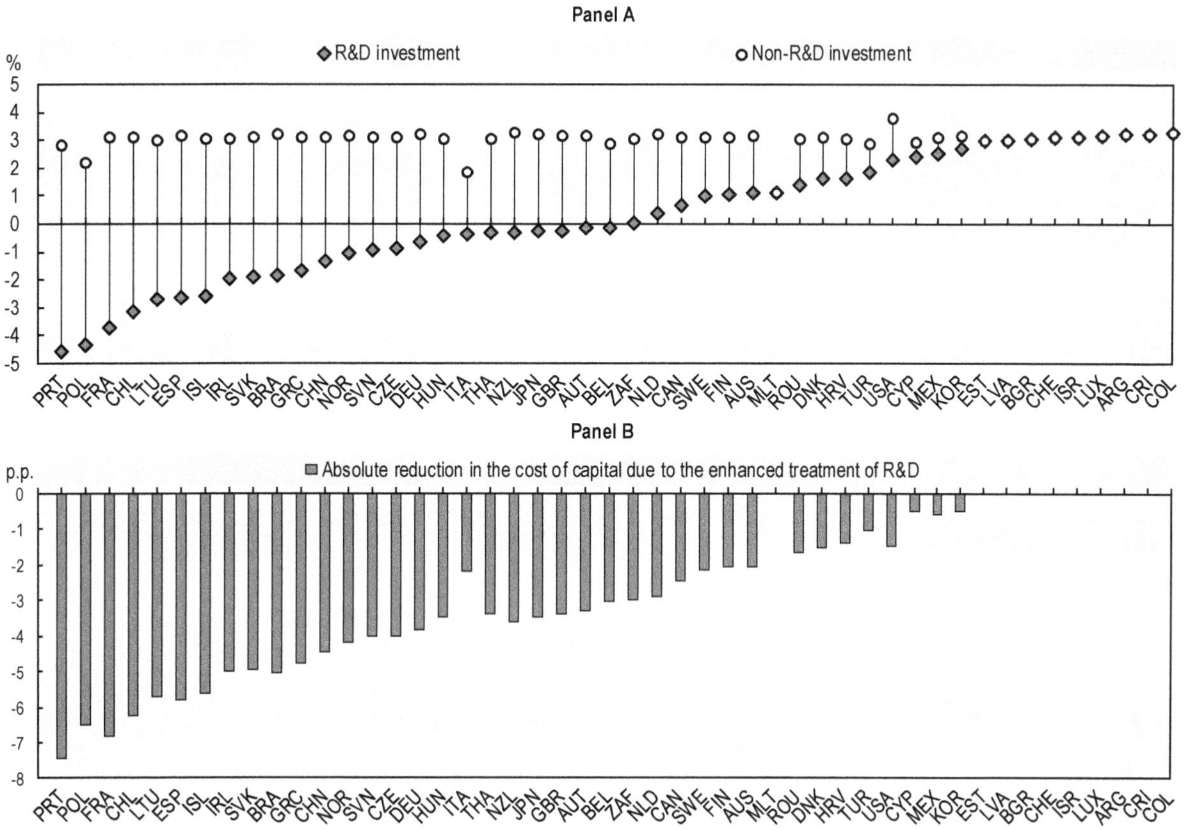

Note: Results refer to a macroeconomic scenario incorporating a 3% real interest rate and a 1% inflation rate and refer to an investment financed by retained earnings including the effect of allowances for corporate equity where available. In the non-R&D case, the cost of capital lies close to the real interest rate due to the large current component in the R&D investment (see Box 5.1), except when an allowance for corporate equity is available.

StatLink https://stat.link/k4z12o

Tax incentives significantly reduce the cost of capital for R&D and while preferential tax treatment has increased since 2019, recent years show a more stable trend. Figure 5.5 compares the evolution of the cost of R&D capital during the period 2019-2023. Similar to the EATR, the cost of capital is affected by changes in the availability of R&D tax incentives and their design. The cost of R&D capital showed a significant decline from an average of 0.4% in 2019 to 0.1% in 2020 and has increased to 0.3% in 2023. Since 2020, the implied tax subsidies have remained relatively stable through 2021, declining slightly in 2022 and 2023. Tax incentives reduced the cost of R&D capital by 94% in 2022 and by 89% in 2023.

The heterogeneity of implied R&D tax subsidy rates

R&D tax benefits may vary with business characteristics such as firm size and profitability. Implied marginal tax subsidy rates for R&D, based on the B-Index indicator (1-B-Index), provide a synthetic indicator of the expected generosity of the tax system towards an extra unit of a firm's R&D investment (Figure 5.6). The more generous the R&D tax incentive is, the greater the value of the implied tax subsidy. This indicator shows differences in tax benefits between large and SMEs and firms in profit and loss-making positions. In jurisdictions, such as Australia or Canada, that offer enhanced tax relief provisions for SMEs that are not available to large firms, the indicator shows the difference in the implied subsidies offered to each firm type.

Figure 5.5. Changing distribution of the average cost of R&D capital, 2019-2023

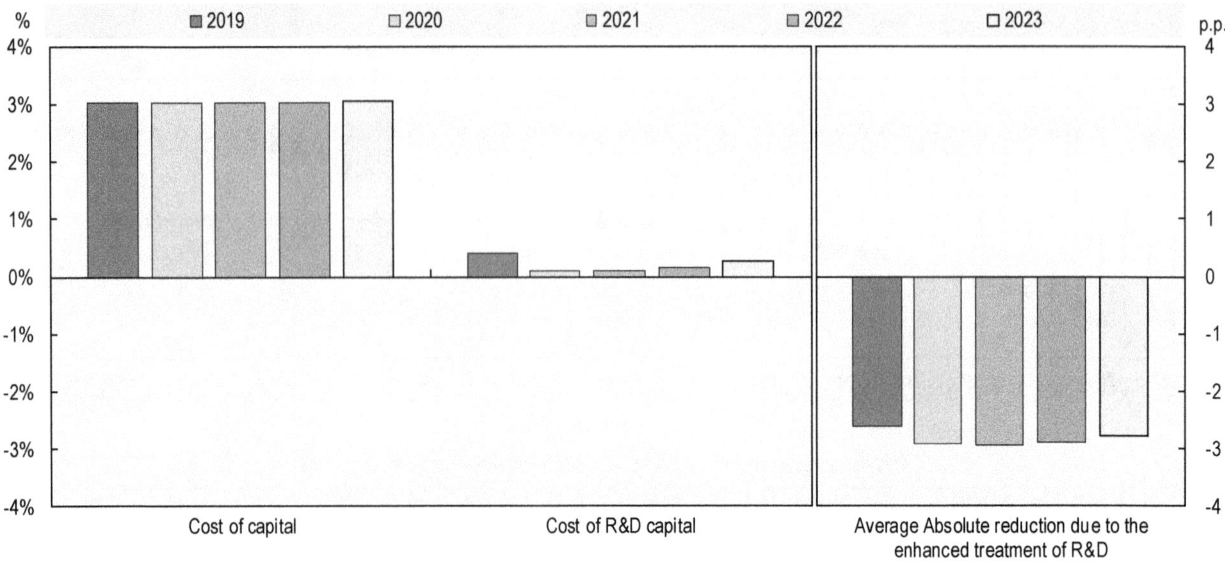

StatLink https://stat.link/ahq4ue

Figure 5.6. Implied marginal tax subsidy rates on business R&D expenditures, 2023

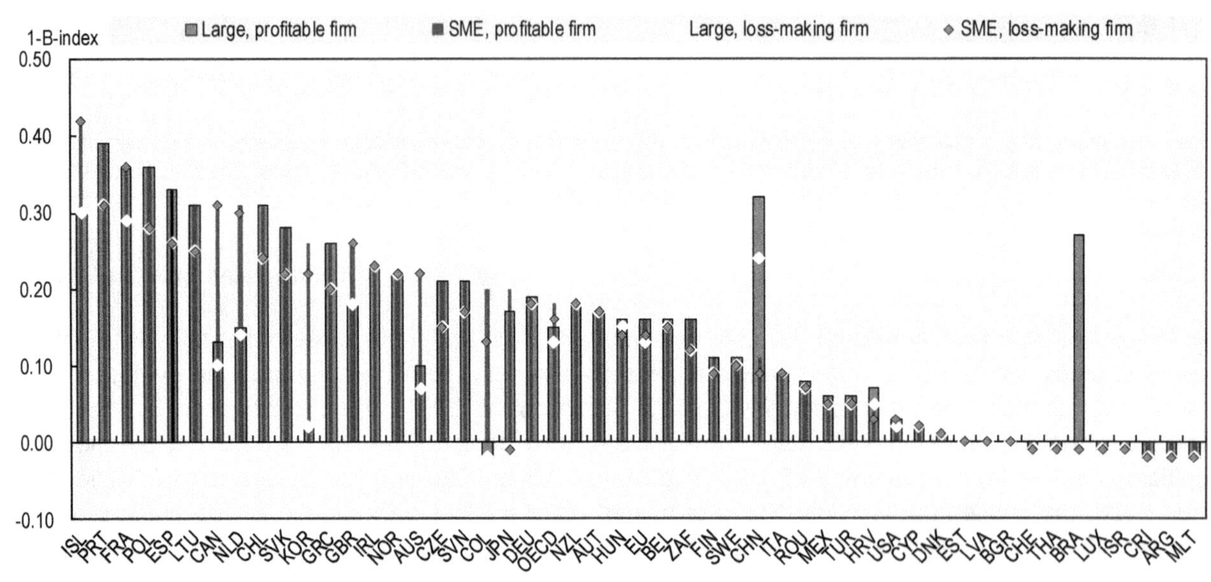

Note: Data and notes: https://oe.cd/ds/rdtax. Modelling assumes a nominal interest rate of 10%.
Source: OECD (2023), R&D Tax Incentive Database, http://oe.cd/rdtax, April 2024, (accessed in May 2024).

StatLink https://stat.link/9e8xlp

Refunds and carry-over provisions are common means of promoting R&D in firms that would not otherwise be able to utilise the support provided by the tax system. This may arise when firms do not have sufficient tax liability to offset earned deductions or do not draw a profit. Implied marginal subsidy rates are calculated under two scenarios: profitable firms (which are able to fully utilise the tax support available to them) and loss-making firms (which may not be able to fully utilise the tax support available to them) to reflect the varying impact of these provisions. Refundability provisions such as those available in Austria and Norway align the subsidy for profitable and loss-making firms. Compared to refunds, carry-over provisions, such as those available in Spain or Portugal, imply a lower subsidy for loss-making firms compared to profitable firms as the benefits may only be used in the future. In jurisdictions where no such provisions exist, such as Brazil or Japan, loss-making firms experience a full loss of tax benefits.

Figure 5.7. Evolution of the implied marginal tax subsidy rates R&D, 2000-2023

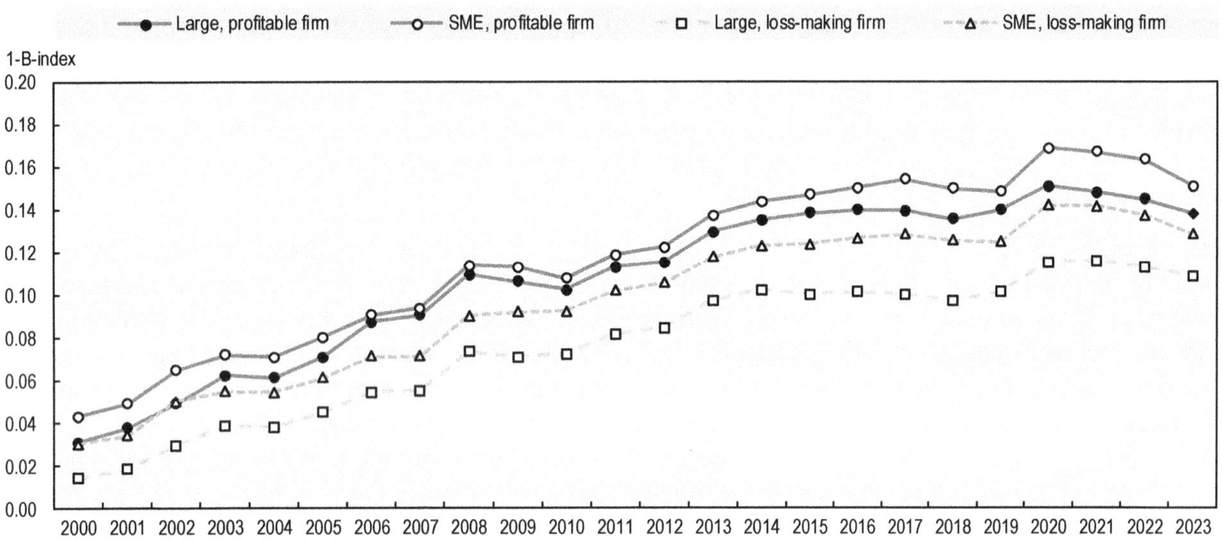

Note: Data and notes: https://oe.cd/ds/rdtax. Modelling assumes a nominal interest rate of 10%.
Source: OECD (2023), R&D Tax Incentive Database, http://oe.cd/rdtax, April 2023, (accessed in September 2023).

StatLink https://stat.link/i1aej7

R&D tax incentives are on average higher for SMEs and profit-making firms. Figure 5.7 offers an overview of the evolution of implied marginal tax subsidy rates across four categories of firms in the period 2000-2023: SMEs and large firms in profit or loss. The generosity of expenditure-based R&D tax incentives rises over time for all firm types. Although between 2013 and 2019 subsidy rates had stabilised, a step increase is observed in 2020. There is some evidence that implied subsidies have declined in recent years. Persistently higher subsidy rates are offered over time to SMEs compared to large firms in both the profit scenarios considered; and to profitable than loss making firms for both firm types. This suggests that jurisdictions tend to provide greater tax benefits to SMEs than large firms.

The evolution of the data depicted in Figure 5.7 also reflects heterogeneity in the magnitude of year-on-year changes. The largest increase in implied marginal tax subsidy rates occurred between 2007-2008, at the time of the financial crisis, (an increase of about 2.0 p.p. throughout all four categories) and 2019-2020 (around 1.6 p.p.), at the time of the COVID pandemic.

Income-based tax incentives

Income-based tax incentives for R&D and innovation feature in the policy mix of many OECD and IF member countries. In 2023, 21 out of 38 OECD countries offer income-based tax incentives to R&D and innovation, representing a substantial increase from 4 countries in 2000. With the exception of Luxembourg, all of these countries offer income-based tax incentives together with expenditure-based tax incentives outlined in the previous section such as R&D tax credits. While expenditure-based tax incentives provide tax relief based on R&D expenditures, income-based tax incentives seek to reduce the taxation of the qualifying income from qualified intangibles resulting from R&D and related activities. They do so by offering a preferential tax rate to the income arising from certain types of R&D intangibles. Income-based tax support can be targeted solely to income from IP assets or extend support to both IP income and other forms of non- IP income (dual category regimes).

The tax treatment of intangible investments varies with firms' decisions on the acquisition, protection and commercialisation of the R&D intangible. This stems from the fact that these tax incentives differ in the types of assets and income they provide relief to and on the conditions that they impose on the development of the asset (González Cabral et al., 2023[4]). The way in which firms acquire an intangible, by doing R&D internally, by outsourcing R&D or by acquiring pre-existing R&D intangible can often determine eligibility for preferential tax relief. The standard tax treatment of costs associated with internally developed R&D intangibles, which are often expensed, is also different from the tax treatment of costs associated with pre-existing intangibles acquired from other firms, which are typically capitalised akin to tangible assets.

The model on which the results in this section are based develops ETRs for different types of approaches through which a firm can come to own an intangible asset (acquired, outsourced or internally generated). Internally generated assets are the focus of the results presented below. The model assumes that the R&D and commercialisation of the R&D intangible occur in the same country. Four key design features of income-based tax incentives are captured: the preferential tax rate, the treatment of ongoing IP expenses, the treatment of past IP expenses and the presence of development conditions through the nexus ratio introduced by Action 5 of the BEPS Project. The model incorporates a gestation lag between the deployment of the R&D investment and the moment the asset starts generating income. The investment is considered to take the form of current expenditure, e.g., the labour costs of hiring researchers, which is in contrast to the expenditure-based incentives where a capital component is incorporated. Additional details on the calibration of the model are contained in González Cabral et. al. (2023[5]).

The main estimates are derived for the case of an intangible asset that is 1) the result of the firms' own R&D, 2) that represents a qualifying intangible asset and 3) that the firm decides to commercialise in the same country (e.g. licenses it out to other domestic performers) or keeps the IP intangible for their own use. When preferential treatment is modelled, the premise is that the asset is deemed to qualify for income-based tax relief and is both a successful investment generating a return. The firm is assumed to have other sources of income (i.e., it is not tax exhausted) and applies for income-based tax support for the first time upon receiving income from the qualifying intangible asset. Where different countries have different income-based tax incentives, these incentives are recorded separately and reported separately unless specified (additional details are provided in González Cabral et. al. (2023[5]) and González Cabral et. al. (2023[6])).

Incentives at the extensive margin

This section develops EATRs for an investment in an internally generated R&D intangible asset, which give insights into the extensive margin of investment decisions, such as firms choosing investment locations across jurisdictions. This provides insights into how the impact of income-based tax incentives may affect the location of the intangible profitable R&D investments. EATRs give insights into the extensive margin of investment decisions, such as firms choosing investment locations across jurisdictions.

At the sample average, income-based tax incentives reduce the overall tax liability that the firm faces on income from an R&D investment substantially, with significant variation across countries (see Figure 5.8). EATRs fall from an average of EATR of 19.6% without support to an EATR of 12.2% including income-based tax incentives. Income-based tax incentives imply a reduction in the EATR by 7.2 percentage points on average, or a reduction of 37%.

The EATR for an income-tax-incentive-supported internally generated R&D investment intangible asset supported through income-based tax incentives ranges from -9% to 30.6% across the countries considered. In the absence of income-based support the rates would vary from 8% to 31%. Among the countries considered, the lowest EATRs are observed in Malta, Israel (ISR1-S, ISR2-S) and Türkiye (TUR1), while the highest rates are observed in Colombia, Brazil and Costa Rica. Countries with the lowest EATR tend to offer the greatest tax-related incentives to investments in internally generated intangibles.

Figure 5.8. EATR for internally generated R&D intangibles, 2023

Estimates of the implied tax subsidy from Income-based tax incentives, inframarginal investments (EATR)

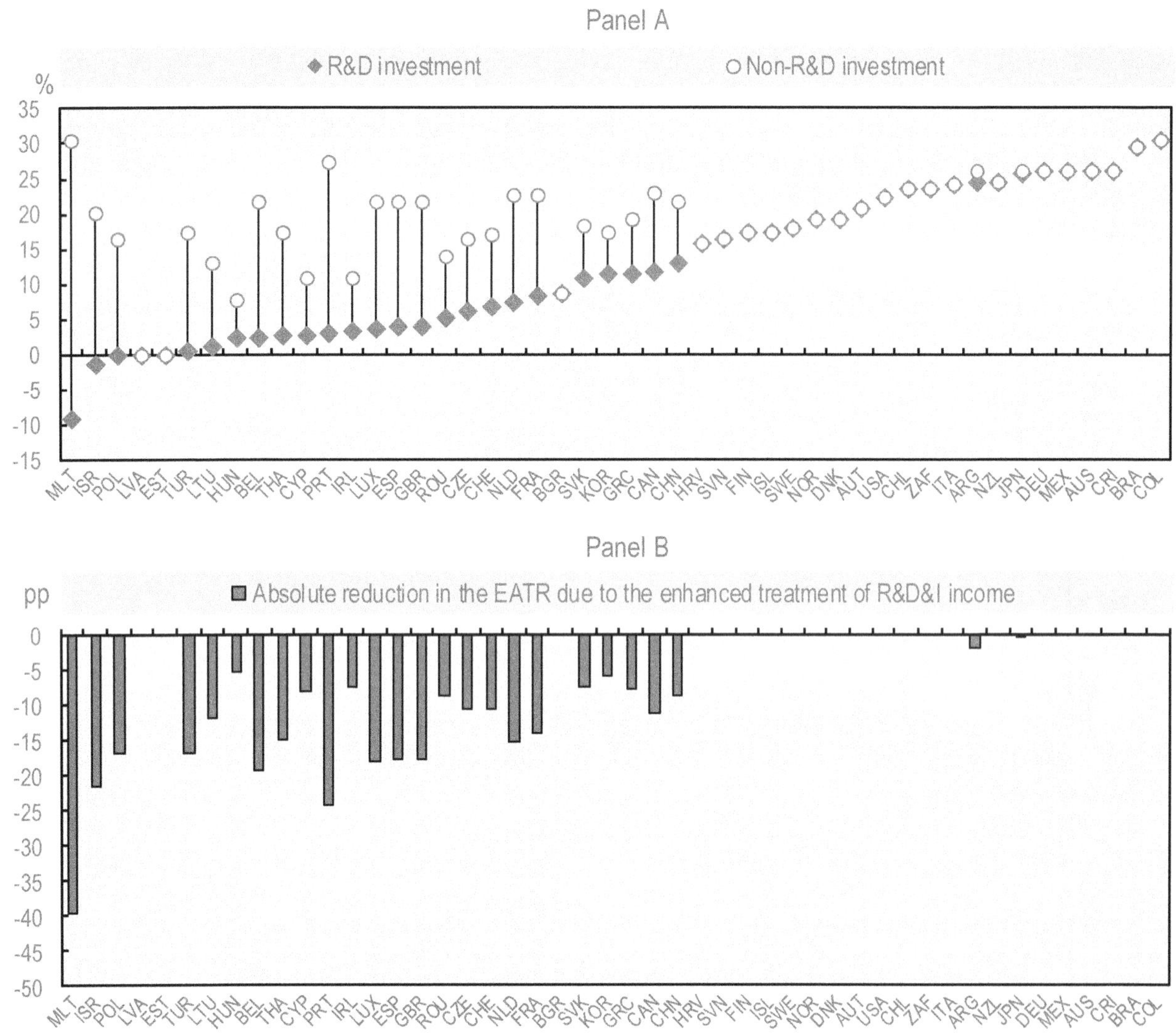

Note: The estimates consider an R&D investment with a gestation lag of two years after which the intangible asset starts generating profits. Baseline refers to an equivalent investment that does not benefit from income-based tax support. Preferential tax treatment is obtained by the difference between the cost of capital including income-based support and the baseline. The results assume all IP income qualifies for relief. CHE assumes that the firm has sufficient other income (non-qualifying IP or non-IP income) that is taxed at higher rates so that it is not subject to the 70% maximum relief limitation. CHE* assume that the maximum relief limitation is binding.

StatLink https://stat.link/4c9xsz

The average taxation of internally generated R&D assets has continuously declined over the past two decades. As shown in Figure 5.9, the average EATR on internally generated R&D intangibles has fallen in the OECD area from 23.3% in 2000 to 12.7% in 2023. The decline stabilises after 2019 and has only been temporarily reversed in two instances; once in 2016 coinciding with the introduction of the BEPS Action 5 minimum standard and in 2022 due to the repeal of an income-based tax incentive in Italy. These trends have to be interpreted in the context of the global fall in STRs, that has led to a reduced taxation of profitable intangible investments even in the absence of income-based tax incentives (Devereux et al., 2002[7]; OECD, 2020[8]). For R&D intangibles that do not benefit from income-based tax incentives, the EATR for OECD countries has fallen from 26.6% in 2000 to 19.5% in 2023, driven by the drop in STRs. Across all 48 countries in the sample, the EATR has fallen from 26.8% in 2000 to 19.5% in 2023. In principle, lower levels of standard taxation could reduce incentives for governments to introduce income-based tax incentives, as the difference between standard and preferential taxation becomes smaller.

Despite falling EATRs under standard taxation, the extent of tax benefits provided to internally generated R&D intangibles has increased on average over time. The green bars in Figure 5.9 display the average implicit tax subsidy granted through Income-based tax incentives as measured by the difference between the average EATR for internally generated R&D intangibles under standard taxation and in the presence of income-based tax incentives. The size of the green bar continues to grow over time even following the introduction of the BEPS Action 5 minimum standard in 2015, but at a slower pace, plateauing after 2019.

Figure 5.9. EATR and implied tax subsidies for internally generated R&D intangibles, OECD countries, 2000-2023

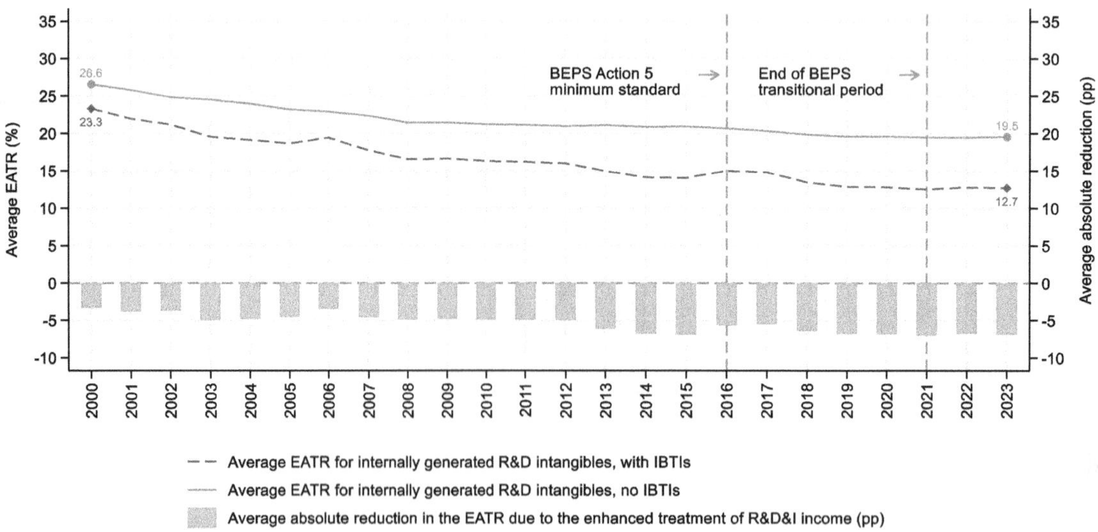

Note: The chart reports the unweighted average EATR across all 38 OECD countries over time, including those that do not offer income-based tax incentives. It accounts for both IP regimes and dual-category regimes. Where income-based tax incentives are available at the central and subnational government level in a given year, only the central level income-based tax incentives enters the OECD average. If several income-based tax incentives are available in the same year, the most generous one is used in the computation of the OECD average. In Canada, income-based tax incentives are only available at the subnational level in the provinces of Québec and Saskatchewan. The regime in the province of Québec is modelled in this average as Québec represents a larger share of Canada's gross domestic product (about twenty percent) relative to Saskatchewan (approximately four percent). In Switzerland, the canton of Nidwalden had an IP regime since 2011. This regime was amended in compliance with the BEPS Action 5 minimum standard in 2016. From 2020, all cantons in Switzerland have the obligation to introduce an IP regime. Estimates for the regime available in the Canton of Nidwalden are not included in this paper due to insufficient data provided to enable the modelling of the regime. Given the federal scope of the new IP regime available since 2020, the estimate for Switzerland is chosen to be that of an investment that takes place in the city of Zurich. The chart includes both IP regimes and dual-category regimes. The estimates consider an R&D investment with a gestation lag of two years after which the intangible asset starts generating profits. Baseline refers to an equivalent investment that does not benefit from income-based tax support. Preferential tax treatment is obtained by the absolute difference between the EATR including income-based support and the baseline.

StatLink https://stat.link/d2lmyq

Incentives at the intensive margin

Income-based tax incentives may also contribute to lower the cost of capital, but this effect is more indirect than for other tax instruments expenditure-based tax incentives. Figure 5.10 shows that while income-based tax incentives have substantially reduced EATRs, they have had much more limited impacts on the cost of capital, which has not declined as sharply over recent years, and where qualifying investments do not enjoy a substantially more preferential treatment compared to other investments. Expenditure-based tax incentives contribute to lowering the cost of capital in a more direct fashion by affecting the cost of investment. The effect of income-based tax incentives to lowering the cost of capital is indirect as they do not affect directly the cost of investing but lower the taxation of future profits. In 2023, income-based tax incentives decreased the cost of capital in OECD countries on average by 0.3 percentage points to an average of 3.9%. The trend over time in the cost of capital for R&D intangible assets has remained relatively stable.

Figure 5.10. Cost of capital of R&D intangibles, OECD countries, 2000-2023

Estimates of the implicit tax subsidy from income-based tax incentives, marginal investments

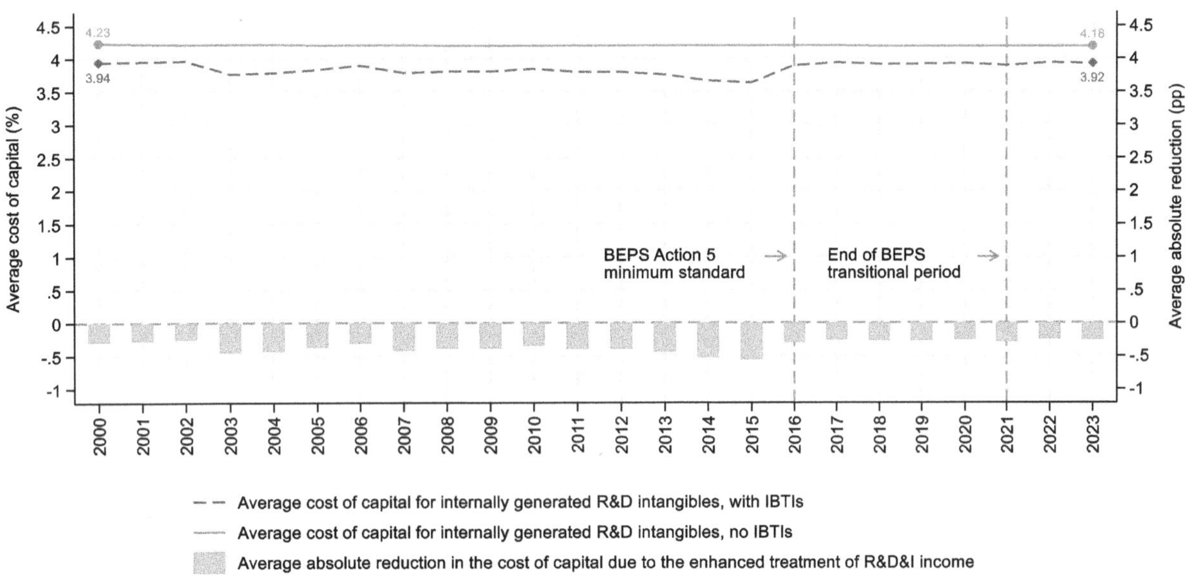

Note: The chart reports the unweighted average cost of capital across all 38 OECD countries over time, including those that do not offer income-based tax incentives. It accounts for both IP regimes and dual-category regimes. Where income-based tax incentives are available at the central and subnational government level in a given year, only the central level income-based tax incentives enters the OECD average. If several income-based tax incentives are available in the same year, the most generous one is used in the computation of the OECD average. In Canada, income-based tax incentives are only available at the subnational level in the provinces of Québec and Saskatchewan. The regime in the province of Québec is modelled in this average as Québec represents a larger share of Canada's gross domestic product (about twenty percent) relative to Saskatchewan (approximately four percent). In Switzerland, the canton of Nidwalden had an IP regime since 2011. This regime was amended in compliance with the BEPS Action 5 minimum standard in 2016. From 2020, all cantons in Switzerland have the obligation to introduce an IP regime. Estimates for the regime available in the Canton of Nidwalden are not included in this paper due to insufficient data provided to enable the modelling of the regime. Given the federal scope of the new IP regime available since 2020, the estimate for Switzerland is chosen to be that of an investment that takes place in the city of Zurich. The chart includes both IP regimes and dual-category regimes. The estimates consider an R&D investment with a gestation lag of two years after which the intangible asset starts generating profits. Baseline refers to an equivalent investment that does not benefit from income-based tax support. Preferential tax treatment is obtained by the absolute difference between the baseline and the cost of capital including income-based support and the baseline.

StatLink https://stat.link/5dzv27

References

Dernis, H. et al. (2019), "World Corporate Top R&D investors: Shaping the Future of Technologies and of AI. A joint JRC and OECD report.", *Publications Office of the European Union*, https://doi.org/10.2760/16575. [2]

Devereux, M. et al. (2002), "Corporate Income Tax Reforms and International Tax Competition", *Economic Policy*, Vol. 17/35, https://www.jstor.org/stable/1344772 (accessed on 29 December 2021). [7]

González Cabral, A., S. Appelt and T. Hanappi (2021), "Corporate effective tax rates for R&D: The case of expenditure-based R&D tax incentives", https://www.oecd-ilibrary.org/taxation/corporate-effective-tax-rates-for-r-d_ff9a104f-en (accessed on 18 February 2023). [3]

González Cabral, A. et al. (2023), "A time series perspective on income-based tax support for R&D and innovation", *OECD Taxation Working Papers*, No. 62, OECD. [6]

González Cabral, A. et al. (2023), *Effective tax rates for R&D intangibles.* [5]

González Cabral, A. et al. (2023), "Design features of income-based tax incentives for R&D and innovation", *OECD Taxation Working Papers*, No. 60, OECD Publishing, Paris, https://doi.org/10.1787/a5346119-en. [4]

OECD (2020), *Tax Challenges Arising from Digitalisation – Economic Impact Assessment: Inclusive Framework on BEPS*, OECD/G20 Base Erosion and Profit Shifting Project, OECD Publishing, Paris, https://doi.org/10.1787/0e3cc2d4-en. [8]

OECD (2022a), *Main Science, Technology and Indicators database.* [1]

OECD (2022b), *R&D Tax Incentive Database*, http://oe.cd/rdtax. [9]

Note

[1] The OECD methodology to compute effective average tax rates for R&D is described in detail in González Cabral, Appelt and Hanappi (2021[3]) and to compute the B-Index is described in OECD (2022b[9]). These indicators also feature in the OECD R&D Tax Incentive database compiled by the OECD Directorate for Science, Technology and Innovation.

6 BEPS Actions

Key insights

- Regarding Action 3, the use of Controlled Foreign Corporation (CFC) rules is widespread, with 53 jurisdictions indicating that CFC rules were in place in 2024, a slight increase from the number in 2019 where 49 jurisdictions had such rules in place.
- Regarding Action 4, the use of Interest Limitation Rules (ILRs) has seen more substantial growth, with 100 in place worldwide amongst IF members, a significant increase from the 67 jurisdictions with them in place in 2019.
- Regarding Action 5, forty-three IP regimes were found to be not harmful, one was found to be potentially harmful but not actually harmful and one was found to be harmful. Six regimes were in the process of being amended or eliminated since they were not compliant with the base erosion and profit shifting (BEPS) Action 5 minimum standard. Ten regimes were abolished by 2024.
- Of the 43 non-harmful intellectual property (IP) regimes, all 43 offer benefits to patents, 32 offer benefits to copyrighted software and 19 offer benefits to the third allowed category of assets that are restricted to small and medium-sized enterprises (SMEs).
- Tax rate reductions for the 43 non-harmful IP regimes range from a full exemption from tax to a reduction of about 40% of the standard tax rate.
- Regarding Action 13, for the fiscal year 2021, 101 jurisdictions have laws in place requiring mandatory filing of CbCRs.
- Five of the six regimes that are in the process of being amended or eliminated offer a full exemption from taxation for IP income.

Introduction

The OECD/G20 BEPS Project was designed to address tax avoidance and double non-taxation of multinational enterprise (MNE) profits by closing gaps that had emerged in the international tax system in the wake of globalisation. The 15 actions of which four are “minimum standards” are designed to equip governments with domestic and international rules and instruments to address tax avoidance, ensuring that profits are taxed where economic activities generating the profits are performed and where value is created.

This chapter contains information on the implementation of four different BEPS Actions worldwide. The Inclusive Framework is moving forward with the implementation of the BEPS minimum standards and continues to peer review the progress of each Inclusive Framework member.

Action 3: Controlled Foreign Company (CFC) Rules

The 2015 BEPS Action 3 report sets out recommended approaches to the development of controlled foreign company (CFC) rules to ensure the taxation of certain categories of MNE income in the jurisdiction of the parent company in order to counter certain offshore structures that result in no or indefinite deferral of taxation. Comprehensive and effective CFC rules have the effect of reducing the incentive to shift profits from a market jurisdiction into a low-tax jurisdiction (Clifford, 2019[1]).

The OECD gathers information on progress related to the implementation of Action 3, namely:

- whether a jurisdiction has CFC rules in place;
- the definition of CFC income;
- whether CFC rules include a substantial economic activity test and, if so, the nature of the test;
- whether any exceptions apply.

This information presented in the *Corporate Tax Statistics* database pertains to the rules in place in 2024.

Figure 6.1. Controlled Foreign Company Rules, 2024

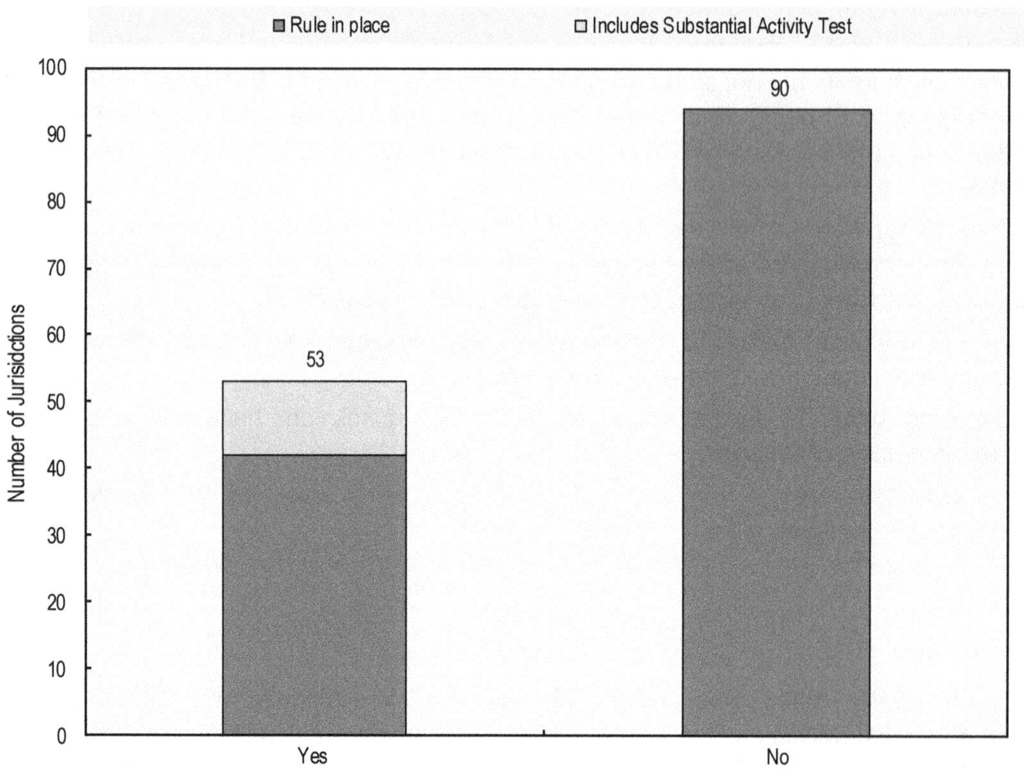

Source: OECD Corporate Tax Survey 2024

StatLink https://stat.link/jku2od

Information on the presence of CFC rules is available for all Inclusive Framework member jurisdictions[1]. Of these, Figure 6.1 shows that 53 jurisdictions indicated that CFC rules were in place in 2024, a slight increase from the number in 2019 where 49 jurisdictions had these rules in place (OECD, 2020[2]). Many jurisdictions may not have a strong need to implement CFC rules as they may not be the UPE jurisdiction of a large number of MNEs.

In general, a CFC is defined as a foreign company that is either directly or indirectly controlled by a resident taxpayer. Jurisdictions apply a variety of criteria to determine control. Some approaches make reference to voting rights held by resident taxpayers or to shareholder value held by resident taxpayers. Others stipulate that a foreign company is a CFC if it carries out its operations in a low-tax jurisdiction. Others base CFC designation on a taxation test (i.e., if the foreign company does not pay tax in its jurisdiction of residence). Jurisdictions also vary in their definitions of CFC income, with some applying CFC rules to any type of income while others apply them to only passive income (i.e., income from interest, rental property, dividends, royalties or capital gains).

Action 4: Interest Limitation Rules (ILR)

The OECD/G20 BEPS project identified the deductibility of interest expense as an important area of attention. In particular, profit shifting can arise from arrangements using third party debt (e.g., where one entity or jurisdiction bears an excessive proportion of the group's total net third party interest expense) and intragroup debt (e.g., where a group uses intragroup interest expense to shift taxable income from high tax to low tax countries).

In response, the 2015 BEPS Action 4 report focused on the use of all types of debt giving rise to excessive interest expense or used to finance the production of exempt or deferred income. In particular, the Action 4 final report established rules that linked an entity's net interest deductions to its level of economic activity within the jurisdiction, measured using taxable earnings before interest income, tax, depreciation and amortisation (EBITDA) (OECD, 2015[3]). This included three main elements:

- A fixed ratio rule based on a benchmark net interest/EBITDA ratio;
- A group ratio rule allowing an entity to deduct more interest expense based on the position of its worldwide group; and
- Targeted rules to address specific risks not addressed by the general rule.

Further work on two aspects of the approach outlined in the Action 4 report was completed in 2017 (OECD, 2016[4]). The first addressed key elements of the design and operation of the group ratio rule, focusing on the calculation of net third party interest expense, the calculation of group-EBITDA and approaches to address the impact of entities with negative EBITDA. The second identified features of the banking and insurance sectors which can constrain the ability of groups to engage in BEPS involving interest, together with limits on these constraints, and approaches to deal with risks posed by entities in these sectors.

The OECD gathers information on progress related to the implementation of Action 4, namely, whether a jurisdiction has an interest limitation rule in place and, if so, the main design features of the rule. Design features include:

- the type of rule (e.g., thin capitalisation, earnings stripping),
- the financial ratio referenced,
- whether the rule is applicable to net or gross interest,
- whether the rule is applicable to related party debt and/or third party debt,
- whether a de minimis threshold is present,
- whether any exclusions apply, and
- whether any loss carry-back or carry-forward provisions apply.

This information is presented in this edition of *Corporate Tax Statistics* and pertains to the rules in place in 2024.

Figure 6.2. Interest Limitation Rule types, 2024

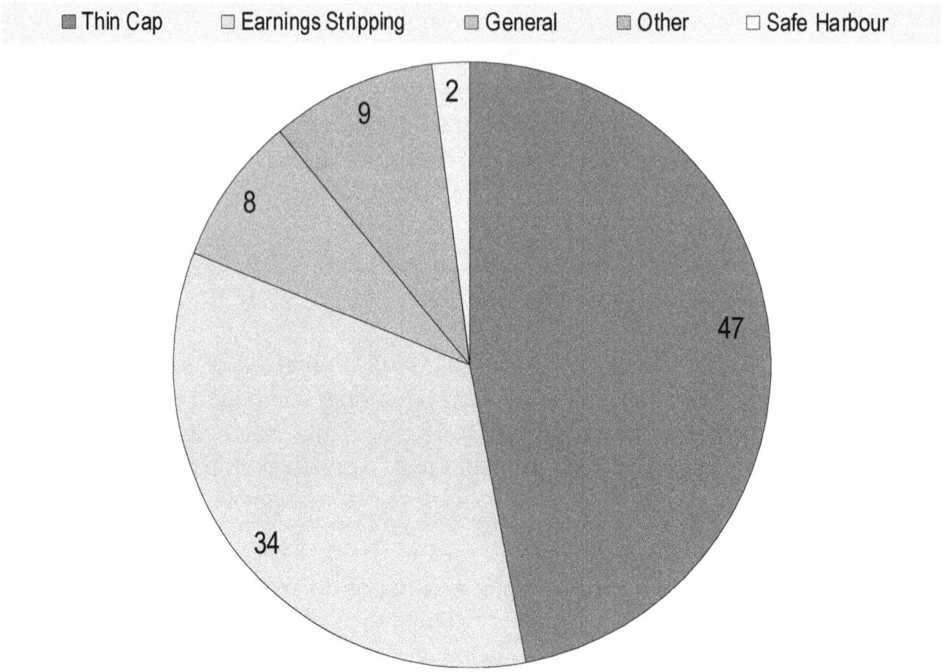

Source: OECD Corporate Tax Survey 2024
Note: Interest Limitation Rules are in place in 100 jurisdictions

StatLink https://stat.link/zne2jx

Information on the presence of interest limitation rules is available for all Inclusive Framework member jurisdictions. Of these, Figure 6.2 shows that 100 indicated that interest limitation rules were in place in 2024. This is a substantial increase from the 67 jurisdictions reporting rules in place for 2019. Of the 100 jurisdictions that had interest limitation rules, the most common involved was thin capitalisation rules (47 jurisdictions), followed by earnings stripping rules (34 jurisdictions).

Thin capitalisation rules disallow the tax deductibility of intra-firm interest payments if the size of these expenses exceeds a threshold, where the threshold is based on debt-to-equity or debt-to-assets ratios. Thin capitalisation rules most commonly reference a debt-to-equity ratio (though a debt-to-assets ratio is used in some jurisdictions), where the ratio values range from 0.3:1 in Brazil (i.e., interest payments are fully deductible only if the indebtedness of the Brazilian borrowing does not exceed 30% of the borrower's net equity) to 6:1 for banks and insurance companies in the Czech Republic, with ratios of 2:1, 3:1 and 4:1 being most common.

Earnings stripping rules restrict tax deductibility if the ratio of interest to EBITDA exceeds a certain threshold. A financial ratio rule based on interest to EBITDA is known as a fixed ratio rule, and is the approach recommended in the Action 4 report. While OECD guidance recommends the use of EBITDA in the denominator, it also allows for the flexibility to introduce rules based on earnings before interest and taxes (EBIT). There may also be interest limitation rules that make reference to other ratios, such as Denmark's rule that applies the ratio of interest to the tax value of total assets. Among the 34 jurisdictions with earnings stripping rules, the most commonly referenced ratio was interest-to-EBITDA (32 jurisdictions), with ratio values ranging from 20% to 50%, with 30% being the most common ratio (27 jurisdictions).

Action 5: Intellectual Property (IP) Regimes

The *Corporate Tax Statistics* database also includes information on IP regimes. Many jurisdictions have implemented IP regimes, which allow income from the exploitation of certain IP assets to be taxed at a lower rate than the standard statutory corporate income tax rate (STR).

IP regimes may be used by governments to support research and development (R&D) activities in their jurisdiction. In the past, IP regimes may have been designed in a manner that incentivised firms to locate IP assets in a jurisdiction regardless of where the underlying R&D activities were undertaken. However, the nexus approach of the BEPS Action 5 minimum standard now requires that tax benefits for IP income are conditional on the extent to which a taxpayer has undertaken the R&D activities that produced the IP asset in the jurisdiction providing the tax benefits.

The information reported for each IP regime in the *Corporate Tax Statistics* database is:

- the name of the regime;
- the qualifying IP assets;
- the reduced rate that applies under the IP regime;
- the status of the IP regime as determined by the OECD's Forum on Harmful Tax Practices (FHTP).

The *Corporate Tax Statistics* database draws on the detailed information collected by the FHTP for its peer reviews of preferential tax regimes. The information and the status presented are correct as of February 2024. Changes to regimes that have been legislated in 2024 but are not effective until 2025 are not reflected in this edition of the database.

What qualifies as an intellectual property regime?

IP regimes can be regimes that exclusively provide benefits to income from IP, but some regimes categorised as IP regimes are "dual category" regimes. These regimes also provide benefits to income from other geographically mobile activities or to a wide range of activities and do not necessarily exclude income from IP.

The *Corporate Tax Statistics* database shows information both on regimes that narrowly target IP income and on regimes that offer reduced rates to IP income and other types of income. Of the 61 IP regimes contained in the database, 34 were reviewed by the FHTP as IP regimes only and 27 were reviewed as "dual category" regimes (IP and non-IP regimes).

Status of intellectual property regimes

On the basis of the features of the regime, IP regimes are found to be either: harmful (because they do not meet the nexus approach), not harmful (when the regime does meet the nexus approach and other factors in the review process), potentially harmful (when the regime does not meet the nexus approach and/or other factors in the review process, but an assessment of the economic effects has not yet taken place), or potentially harmful but not actually harmful (when the regime does not meet the nexus approach and/or other factors in the review process, but an assessment of the economic effects has taken place). Regimes may also be in the process of being amended or eliminated (when the regime may not meet the nexus approach and/or other factors in the review process and is being modified or abolished as a result). The peer review process is ongoing, and by 2024 the vast majority of regimes were fully aligned with the Action 5 minimum standard. These are listed with the status "Not harmful" or "amended (not harmful)". Regimes that were already closed to new entrants in 2024 (according to the peer reviews approved by the Inclusive Framework in February 2024) were listed as "abolished" in the database, although continuing benefits may be offered for a defined period of time to companies already benefiting from the regime. In most cases, this grandfathering would end by 30 June 2024. There were ten IP regimes listed as abolished in 2024.

The *Corporate Tax Statistics* database contains information on 61 IP regimes that were in place in 46 different jurisdictions in the year 2024 as shown in Figure 6.3. Forty-three regimes in total were found to be not harmful; 26 of these regimes were found to be not harmful after having been amended to align with the Action 5 minimum standard. One regime was found to be potentially harmful but not actually harmful (in Brunei Darussalam) and one regime (in Trinidad and Tobago) was found to be harmful. Six regimes are in the process of being amended or eliminated.

Figure 6.3. Status of intellectual property regimes in place in 2024

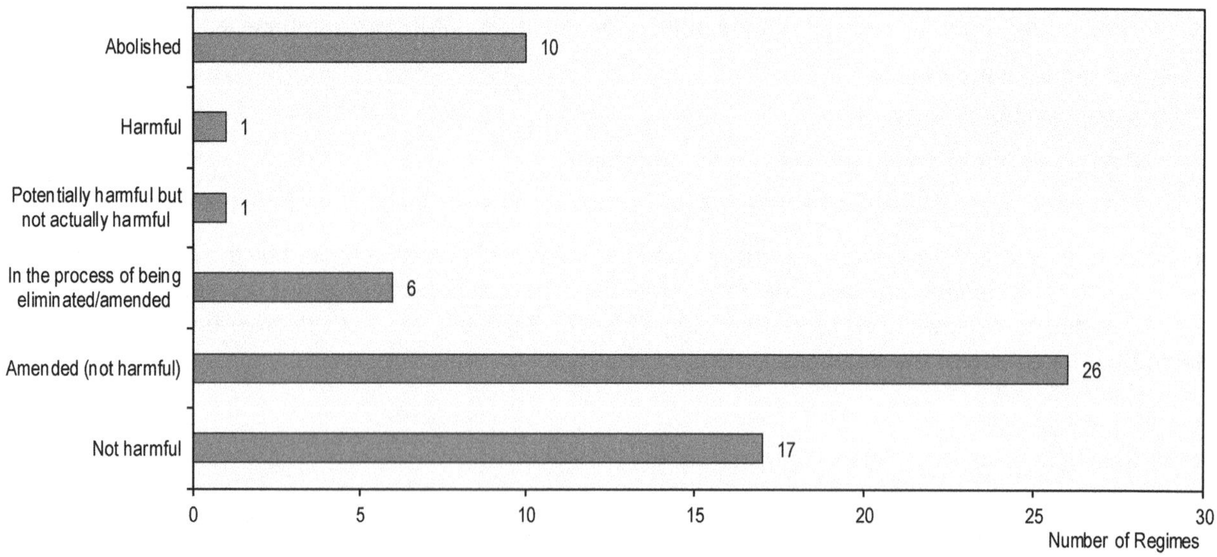

Source: OECD Forum on Harmful Tax Purposes

StatLink https://stat.link/vi6bgq

Qualifying assets and reduced tax rates

In the *Corporate Tax Statistics* database, qualifying assets of IP regimes are grouped into three main categories: patents, software and Category 3. These correspond to the only three categories of assets that may qualify for benefits under the Action 5 minimum standard: 1) patents defined broadly; 2) copyrighted software; and 3) in certain circumstances and only for SMEs, other IP assets that are non-obvious, useful and novel. The Action 5 Report explicitly excludes income from marketing related intangibles (such as trademarks) from benefiting from a tax preference. If a regime does not meet the Action 5 minimum standard, then the assets qualifying for the regime may not fall into the three allowed categories.

Of the 43 regimes found to be not harmful, all 43 regimes cover patents, 32 cover software, and 19 regimes cover assets in the third category (Category 3). All seven regimes that are in the process of being eliminated or amended do not have any restrictions on the type of income that qualifies for a reduced rate, although other restrictions may apply, (e.g. to certain industries). The reduction in the rate on IP income varies among the regimes, and some regimes offer different rates depending, for example, on the type of income (e.g., royalties or capital gains income) or size of the company.

Among the 43 regimes found to be not harmful, the tax benefit offered ranges from a full exemption to a reduction of about 40% of the tax rate that would have otherwise applied. The most common reduction is a 50% reduction. The reduced rates range from 0% (in 13 jurisdictions) to 18.75% (Korea's Special taxation for transfer, acquisition, etc. of technology; this IP regime offers reduced rates ranging from 5% to 18.75%). Five of the six regimes that are in the process of being amended or eliminated offer a full exemption from taxation for IP income.

For each of the 43 non-harmful IP regimes, Figure 6.4 and Figure 6.5 show the lowest reduced rate offered under the regime and the tax rate that would otherwise apply. Figure 6.4 shows those regimes with the status non-harmful, while Figure 6.5 shows the regimes that have been amended to be non-harmful. The tax rate that would otherwise apply is typically the STR, but it may not include certain surtaxes or sub-central government taxes. Similar to the reduced rate, the tax rate that would otherwise apply may also fall into a range, for example, if the standard statutory rate depends on the level of profits. Therefore, the tax rates shown in the figures are illustrative and do not detail the full range of tax reductions offered in each IP regime.

Figure 6.4. Reduced rates under non-harmful intellectual property regimes, 2024

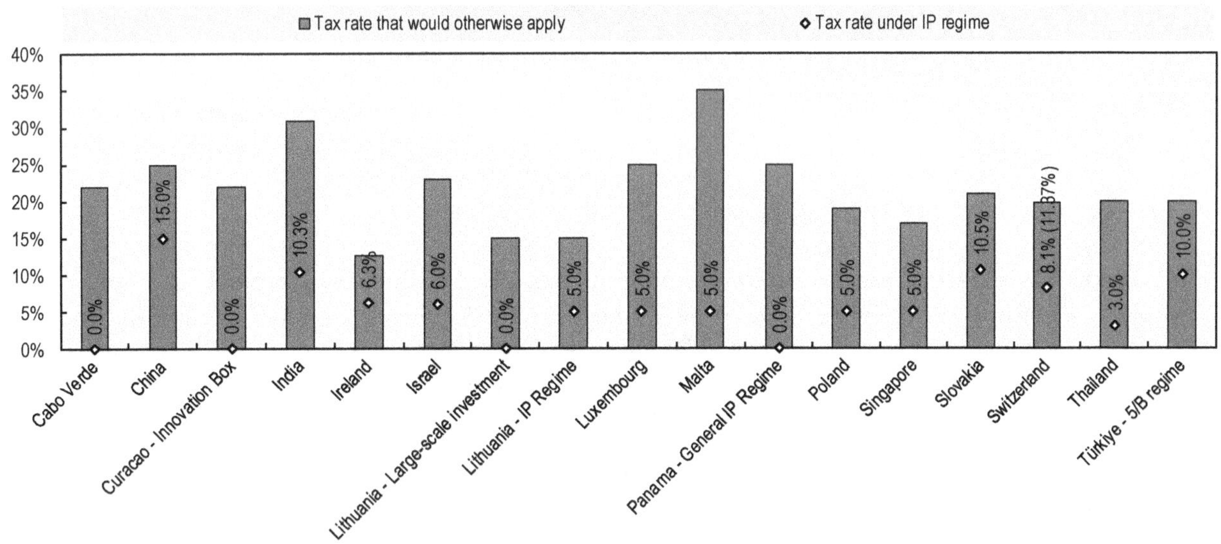

Note: IP income in Switzerland can benefit from a 90% exemption of qualifying IP income from cantonal taxation. However, this exemption is subject to a cap: only 70% of a firm's total profits (IP or non-IP) can be exempt. The canton of Zurich is chosen as the representative canton. The 8.11% in 2024 applies to qualifying IP income and assumes that the firm has sufficient other income (non-qualifying IP or non-IP income) that is taxed at higher rates so that it is not subject to the 70% maximum relief limitation. If the firm had enough qualifying IP income that the 70% maximum relief limitation did apply, the rate applied to IP income in the city of Zurich would increase steadily from 8.11% to 11.37% in 2024 (100% IP Income). Where multiple rates are available for royalties or capital gains, the rate applicable to royalties has been used.

StatLink https://stat.link/jnwb75

Figure 6.5. Reduced rates under non-harmful (amended) intellectual property regimes, 2024

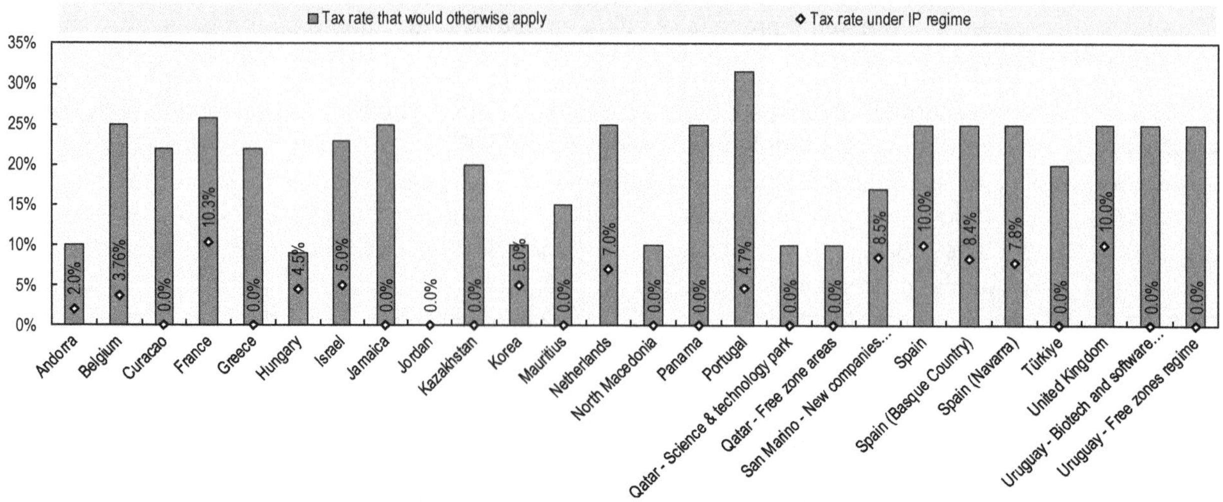

Note: Where multiple rates are available for royalties or capital gains, the rate applicable to royalties has been used.

StatLink https://stat.link/fga2et

Action 13: Country-by-Country Reporting (CbCR) implementation

BEPS Action 13 is part of the transparency pillar of the OECD/G20 BEPS project. In many cases, jurisdictions already have rules in place to deal with BEPS risks posed by MNE groups but may not previously have had access to information to identify cases where these risks arise. BEPS Action 13 helps to address this by providing new information for use by tax administrations in high-level transfer pricing risk assessment and the assessment of other BEPS-related risks.

For the fiscal year 2022, 102 jurisdictions have laws in place requiring mandatory filing of Country-by-Country Reports (CbCRs). (Figure 6.6).

Feedback from tax administrations indicates that they are using CbCRs to combat BEPS, in combination with other tools: (i) to help identify MNE groups for possible audit, (ii) to help identify MNE groups that do not need to be audited (de-selection), and (iii) to help plan audits or other enquiries. The specific approaches adopted vary depending upon each tax administration's general approach to risk assessment. Two important points to note on the role of CbCRs include:

- **CbCRs may only be used in a high-level risk assessment of an MNE.** CbCRs may not be used as evidence that BEPS exists or as a substitute for substantive enquiries and should be used alongside other information available to tax administrations. It is unlikely that success in particular cases will be able to be attributed to CbCRs specifically.
- **There may be a significant time delay between a CbCR being filed and the outcomes of a transfer pricing audit.** CbCRs may be used for the purposes of a high-level risk assessment and in planning a tax audit, but it will only be determined whether an MNE group is in fact engaged in BEPS once further enquiries are completed, which may take a number of years.

While CbCRs are an important tool, tax administrations are using them in concert with a range of other tools in their efforts to combat BEPS. The OECD has developed several tools to support tax administrations in using CbCRs and, in particular, in undertaking multilateral activity to risk assess MNE groups. These include regular CbCR risk assessment workshops; the CbCR Tax Risk Evaluation and Assessment Tool (TREAT) for tax administrations; a Tax Risk Assessment Questionnaire (TRAQ), which is used in the

International Compliance Assurance Programme (ICAP) provided by a tax administration to an MNE group with an invitation to explain key indicators of possible risk; and the CbCR Effective Risk Assessment Handbook, released in 2017.

The number of jurisdictions providing aggregated and anonymised CbCR statistics has increased yearly since their introduction in 2016. Figure 6.7 shows that the total number of jurisdictions that could potentially provide CbCR statistics to the OECD increased from 58 in 2016 to 102 in 2022. This total is calculated as the number of jurisdictions that have implemented mandatory CbCR filing along with those that accepted voluntary filing in the specific year. For example, in 2016, 49 jurisdictions implemented mandatory filing while a further 9 accepted voluntary filing. The number of jurisdictions that provided CbCR statistics increased from 26 to 52 over the same period. Despite the large increase in the number of jurisdictions that could potentially submit CbCR statistics the number of jurisdictions that did not provide CbCR statistics to the OECD has only increased from 32 to 44 with an additional five jurisdictions reporting that they have received zero CbCRs in 2021. Many jurisdictions receive too few CbCRs to be able to provide the statistics under their confidentiality standards.

Figure 6.6. Number of jurisdictions implementing mandatory CbCR filing

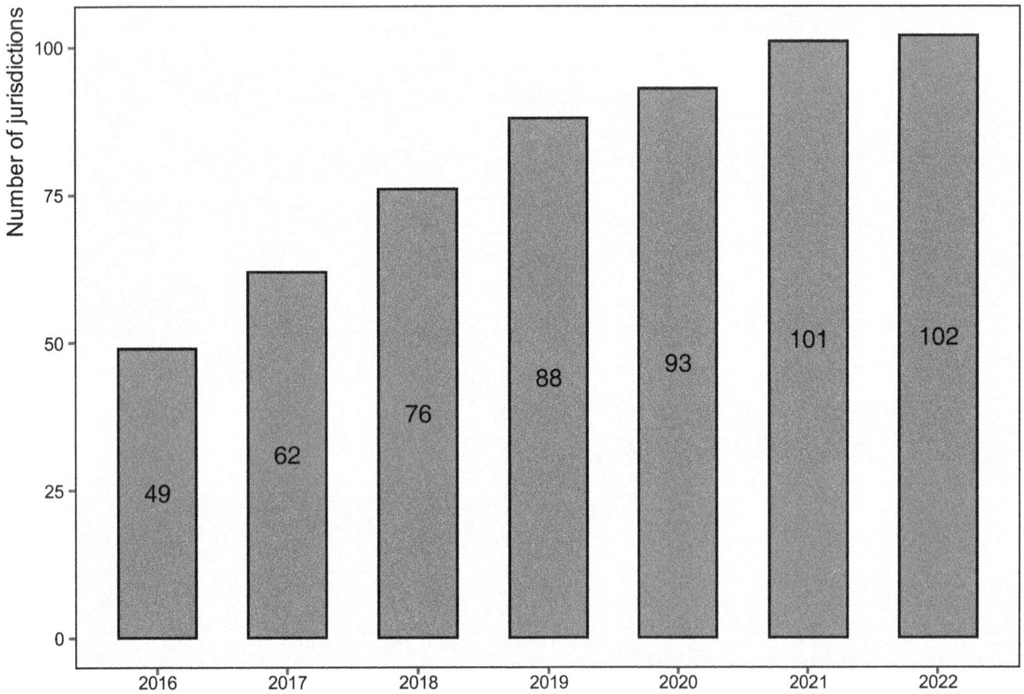

Source: Action 13 Automatic exchange portal (https://oe.cd/3Kj).

StatLink https://stat.link/plfzw8

Figure 6.7. The evolution of CbCR coverage

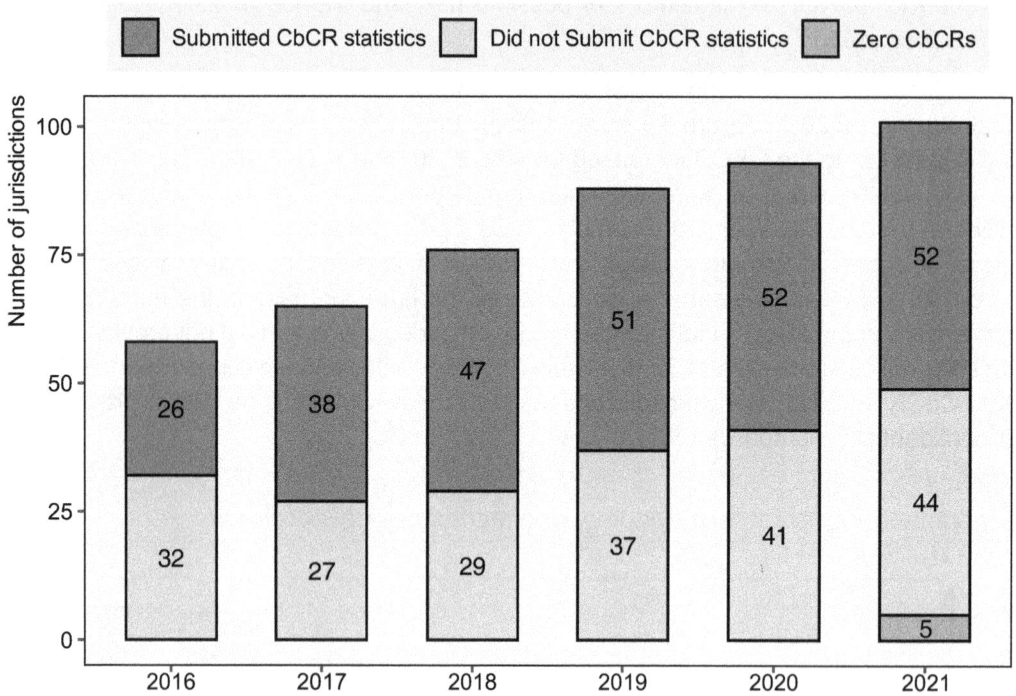

Source: Anonymised and Aggregated CbCR statistics and OECD Country-by-Country Reporting Requirements.

StatLink https://stat.link/dlqyav

References

Clifford, S. (2019), "Taxing multinationals beyond borders: Financial and locational responses to CFC rules", *Taxing multinationals beyond borders: Financial and locational responses to CFC rules*, https://doi.org/10.1016/j.jpubeco.2019.01.010. [1]

OECD (2020), *Corporate Tax Statistics, Second Edition*, OECD Publishing, Paris, https://doi.org/10.1787/ff4d4ce8-en. [2]

OECD (2016), *Limiting Base Erosion Involving Interest Deductions and Other Financial Payments, Action 4 - 2016 Update: Inclusive Framework on BEPS*, OECD/G20 Base Erosion and Profit Shifting Project, OECD Publishing, Paris, https://doi.org/10.1787/9789264268333-en. [4]

OECD (2015), *Limiting Base Erosion Involving Interest Deductions and Other Financial Payments, Action 4 - 2015 Final Report*, OECD/G20 Base Erosion and Profit Shifting Project, OECD Publishing, Paris, https://doi.org/10.1787/9789264241176-en. [3]

Note

[1] Covers 143 IF members as of the 1st January 2024.

7 Country-by-country reporting statistics

Key insights

- The 2024 edition of *Corporate Tax Statistics* contains a further year of anonymised and aggregated country-by-country reporting (CbCR) statistics covering fiscal year (FY) 2021.
- Fifty-two jurisdictions out of a potential one hundred and one submitted CbCR statistics to the OECD detailing the financial and business activities of over 8000 multinational enterprises (MNEs), with a further five jurisdictions reporting that they received zero CbCRs.
- Data for FY 2021 show a modest reduction between the location where profits are reported and the location where economic activities occur. Revenues and profits per employee remain higher in investment hubs, though these ratios are decreasing. For example, the data show that the median value of revenues per employee in investment hubs is USD 1 640 000 as compared to just USD 330 000 for all other jurisdictions. This value for hubs has however declined from USD 2 000 000 in 2017.
- The data includes a jurisdiction-by-jurisdiction breakdown of low-taxed profit of MNEs (defined as profit taxed at an effective tax rate below 15%) headquartered in some jurisdictions. This data highlights the presence of low-taxed profit in low-tax and high-tax jurisdictions alike, with more than half of the low-taxed profit in the new data located in jurisdictions with average effective tax rates (ETRs) above 15%.
- In FY 2021 there is a large increase in overall total profits of the MNEs covered which could be attributed to recovery following the COVID-19 pandemic or to recent increases in inflation in many IF member jurisdictions.
- The composition of business activity differs across jurisdiction groups. The most predominant activity in investment hubs is "holding shares" which also includes other equity instruments.

Country-by-country reporting was implemented as part of Action 13 of the OECD/G20 BEPS Project to support jurisdictions in combating base erosion and profit shifting (BEPS). Under BEPS Action 13, all large multinational enterprises (MNEs) are required to prepare a country-by-country (CbC) report with aggregate data on the global allocation of income, profit, taxes paid and economic activity for all tax jurisdictions in which it operates. This CbC report is shared with tax administrations in these jurisdictions, for use in high level transfer pricing and BEPS risk assessments.

While the main purpose of CbCRs is to support tax administrations in the high-level detection and assessment of transfer pricing and other BEPS-related risks, data collected from CbCRs can also play a role in supporting the economic and statistical analysis of BEPS activity and of multinational enterprises in general. Under Action 11 of the BEPS Project (OECD, 2015[1]), acknowledging the need for additional sources of data on MNEs, jurisdictions agreed to regularly publish anonymised and aggregated CbCR statistics to support the ongoing economic and statistical analysis of MNE activities and BEPS. This section outlines progress on the implementation of Action 13, as well as the country-by-country reporting statistics published by the OECD under Action 11.

General CbCR data characteristics

Jurisdictions have provided the OECD with anonymised and aggregated tabulations of the country-by country reporting information described below. Aggregation is performed at the sub-group level according to certain sub-group or group characteristics and reported according to these different criteria in several tables (see Box 7.1). Table 7.1 provides an overview of the tables submitted to the OECD as part of CbCR statistics, a brief description of their content and the number of individual jurisdictions that submitted each table for FY 2021.

The aggregated CbCR data are subject to a number of limitations that need to be borne in mind when carrying out any economic or statistical analysis (see Box 7.2). Nonetheless, the data provide important information on MNEs and their activities relative to previously existing data sources:

- The CbCR data provide global information on MNEs' activities, with more granular information than is available in other data sources such as consolidated financial accounts.[1]
- The CbCR data include information on number of CbCRs, number of sub-groups, number of entities, total unrelated and related party revenues (and their sum, total revenues), profit or loss before income tax, income tax paid (on a cash basis), current year income tax accrued, stated capital, accumulated earnings, number of employees, tangible assets other than cash and cash equivalents, and the main business activity (or activities) of each constituent entity.
- The data ensure inclusion of all global activities of included MNEs.
- At a minimum, the data allows for the domestic and foreign activities of MNEs to be separately identified.[2] Depending on the reporting jurisdiction, it allows for an analysis of MNEs' activities in investment hubs and developing jurisdictions thanks to a detailed geographical disaggregation.
- Information is reported by jurisdiction of tax residence and not jurisdiction of incorporation.
- The CbCR data provide cross-country information on MNEs' business activities (e.g., manufacturing, intellectual property (IP) holding, sales) in different jurisdictions, allowing researchers to relate financial outcomes to these functions for the first time.

The CbCR data thus provide governments and researchers with important new information to analyse MNE behaviour, particularly in relation to tax, allowing for the construction of a more complete view of the global activities of the largest MNEs than is possible using existing sources.

The anonymised and aggregated CbCR statistics are constructed in two main steps. First, all large MNEs (i.e., with consolidated revenues of at least EUR 750 million) file CbCRs, typically with the tax administration in the jurisdiction of their ultimate parent entity (UPE). An MNE group is usually required to file its CbCR one year after the closing date of its fiscal year. Second, in each jurisdiction, tax administrations or other government bodies compile the different CbCR filings into a single dataset according to their specific confidentiality standards. This results in a single anonymised and aggregated dataset covering all the jurisdiction's MNEs subject to the filing requirement, which is shared with the OECD.

Box 7.1. MNE group structure

An **MNE group** is a collection of enterprises related through ownership or control such that the group is either required to prepare consolidated financial statements for financial reporting purposes under applicable accounting principles or would be so required if equity interests in any of the enterprises were traded on a public securities exchange.

An **entity** is any separate business unit of an MNE group that is included in the consolidated financial statements of the MNE group for financial reporting purposes.

The **UPE** directly or indirectly owns a sufficient interest in one or more other entities of the MNE group such that it is required to prepare consolidated Financial Statements.

A **sub-group** is formed by the combined entities of an MNE group operating in one tax jurisdiction.

Table 7.1. Content of anonymised and aggregated CbCR statistics

CbCR table	Content	Description
Table 1A	Aggregate totals of all variables by jurisdiction	Reports variable totals and selected ratios for all sub-groups, obtained by aggregating sub-group variables according to their jurisdiction of tax residence (or jurisdiction groups, depending on confidentiality). The tables include three panels aggregating all sub-groups, sub-groups with positive profits and sub-groups with negative profits.
Table 1B	Interquartile mean values of all variables by jurisdiction	Reports interquartile mean figures based on the number of CbCR sub-groups following the same structure as Table 1A.
Table 4	Aggregate totals of all variables by effective tax rate of MNE groups	Reports data disaggregated by effective tax rate of the MNE group and by tax jurisdiction. The level of disaggregation varies across jurisdictions, depending on confidentiality.
Table 5	Aggregate totals of all variables by effective tax rate of MNE sub-groups	Reports data disaggregated by the effective tax rate of the MNE sub-group. The level of disaggregation varies across jurisdictions, depending on confidentiality.
Table 6	Distribution points of MNE group size	Reports distribution points of MNE group size, as measured by unrelated party revenues, number of employees and tangible assets. The total size of an MNE group is determined by summing the relevant variables across all of its sub-groups.

Note: The collection of Table 2, where the data is aggregated according to the MNEs size, will commence from FY 2022. The collection of Table 3, where the data is aggregated according to the MNEs sector has been postponed. The Inclusive Framework will consider whether to expand the dataset to include Table 3 in future years. The ETR of the MNE group and sub-group in Tables 4 and 5 should not be directly compared to the effective tax rates mentioned in the chapter on corporate effective tax rates.

Coverage of CbCR statistics

While there are 143 members of the Inclusive Framework, 101 have implemented mandatory reporting for the FY 2021. Fifty-two jurisdictions submitted CbCR statistics to the OECD with a further five jurisdictions reporting that they received zero CbCRs in 2021. The 2024 edition of *Corporate Tax Statistics* includes CbCR statistics on CbCRs filed in 52 headquarter jurisdictions, covering over 8 000 MNE groups (see Table 7.2). This dataset contains a vast array of information on the global financial and economic activities of MNEs.

Anonymised and aggregated CbCR data provide an overview of where large MNE groups are headquartered. Table 7.2 shows that, across the jurisdictions that submitted data, the United States and

Japan host one third of the headquarters of MNEs included in the sample. The number of reported MNEs varies considerably among jurisdictions, ranging from a minimum of two in Morocco to 1 791 in the United States. The median number of reported MNEs per jurisdiction is 69. 355 MNEs filed CbCRs as surrogate parent entities (where the jurisdiction of tax residence is different from the UPE's jurisdiction of tax residence in cases where CbCR reporting rules may not be in place in the UPE's jurisdiction of tax residence). Jurisdictions provided detailed statistics for 279 out of the 355 CbCRs that were filed.

The number of headquarter MNEs covered in the CbCR statistics has increased over time, from 3 628 in 2016 to 7 628 in 2021[3]. Panel A of Figure 7.1 shows the breakdown of these MNE headquarters by regional grouping. There is a fairly even split of headquarter locations between the Americas, Asia & Oceania and Europe across the sample. However, Panel B of Figure 7.1 shows that in general, MNEs in Asia & Oceania host more business entities than in the other regional groupings.

Box 7.2. Limitations of the CbCR data and actions to improve the quality of the data

The aggregated CbCR data are subject to a number of limitations that need to be borne in mind when carrying out any economic or statistical analysis. Some limitations include that:

- Much of the data is too aggregated to allow detailed investigation of specific BEPS channels (e.g., there is no distinction between royalties and interest in related party payments, and no information on intangible assets).
- Often but not always, CbCRs are based on financial accounting data.[1] Due to differences between financial and other permitted accounting rules and tax reporting rules, CbCR data might not accurately represent how items are reported for tax purposes. Differences in accounting rules could affect the comparability of CbCR data across jurisdictions.
- There are a number of data deficiencies described in the disclaimer accompanying the data, which is available at http://www.oecd.org/tax/tax-policy/anonymised-and-aggregated-cbcr-statistics-disclaimer.pdf. In the absence of specific guidance, MNEs may have included intra-company dividends in profit figures, meaning that profit figures could be subject to double counting.
- While the inclusion of dividends in the profit figure is normal in separate financial accounting, in the context of corporate income tax analysis it can lead to biased results. For example, the tax treatment of repatriated dividends can differ across jurisdictions. As a distribution of post-tax profits, dividends are often lightly taxed or tax exempt.[2] To evaluate the potential magnitude of included dividends, some jurisdictions have carried out their own independent analyses of this question.[3]
- In the case of stateless entities, the inclusion of transparent entities such as partnerships may give rise to double counting of revenue and profit. On the other hand, the data may imply that stateless profit are untaxed, since this income is generally taxed at the level of the owner.
- Corporate income tax (CIT) exempt companies such as pension funds or university hospitals are required to file CbCRs and as such are included in aggregated statistics, unless otherwise specified. The inclusion of these companies could distort the relationship between profits and taxes.

Some of the data limitations have already been addressed through revised guidance. For example, with respect to the double-counting of dividends, the guidance on CbCR implementation was updated in November 2019 to specify that intra-company dividends should be excluded from profit figures. However, because of the time lag in the revision of instructions with jurisdictions and in reporting, it is expected to take several years before these actions lead to improvements in data quality. Other issues, e.g., the treatment of stateless entities, are the subject of ongoing discussion, including through the review of Country-by-Country Reporting (BEPS Action 13)[4] that could lead to the collection of more detailed information through CbCR reports in the future. The OECD continues to work with members of the Inclusive Framework and other stakeholders to improve the quality and consistency of the data across jurisdictions. In light of these potential improvements, it is expected that the value and importance of the dataset in providing researchers and the public with a valuable tool for better understanding the global activities of MNEs and BEPS will continue to increase over time.

In addition to the limitations mentioned above, caution needs to be exercised when attempting to draw conclusions from the data for several reasons:

- Changes and potential trends in BEPS behaviour cannot be detected with a single year of data.
- In the short term, comparability between the 2016 and subsequent samples is limited, e.g., because of the move from voluntary to mandatory filing and differences in fiscal year coverage.[5] In the longer term, changes to guidance will lead to changing treatment of some variables such as profits, also limiting the comparison of these variables over time.
- Even with additional years of data, a number of other events that affect the data may make it difficult to identify the effect of BEPS-related policies (e.g., COVID-19, and the United States' 2017 Tax Cuts and Jobs Act).
- Implementing BEPS measures takes time, and the effects of these measures may not become evident until a few years after implementation.

1. Reporting MNEs may choose to use data from consolidation reporting packages, from separate entity statutory financial statements, regulatory financial statements, or internal management accounts. In some jurisdictions, taxpayers are permitted to use financial statements or records maintained for tax reporting purposes.
2. In the European Union, the Council directive 2011/96/EU limits the ability of EU Member States to tax received dividends in order to exempt dividends and other profit distributions paid by subsidiary companies to their parent companies from withholding taxes and to eliminate double taxation of such income at the level of the parent company.
3. Country specific analysis undertaken by Ireland, Italy, the Netherlands, Sweden and the United Kingdom are available at: Ireland: https://oe.cd/3Kn; Italy: https://oe.cd/3Ko; Netherlands: https://oe.cd/3Kp; Sweden: https://oe.cd/3Kq; United Kingdom: https://oe.cd/3Kr.
4. The BEPS Action 13 report (http://www.oecd.org/tax/transfer-pricing-documentation-and-country-by-country-reporting-action-13-2015-final-report-9789264241480-en.htm) included a requirement that a review of the CbCR minimum standard be completed (the 2020 review). A public consultation meeting on the 2020 review of BEPS Action 13 was held virtually on 12-13 May 2020, where external stakeholders had the opportunity to provide input on the ongoing work.
5. The 2017 data and future releases cover fiscal years ending between 1 January and 31 December of the respective year while the 2016 data contains CbCRs for fiscal years starting between 1 January and 1 July 2016.

Figure 7.1. Distribution of MNEs and entities by region

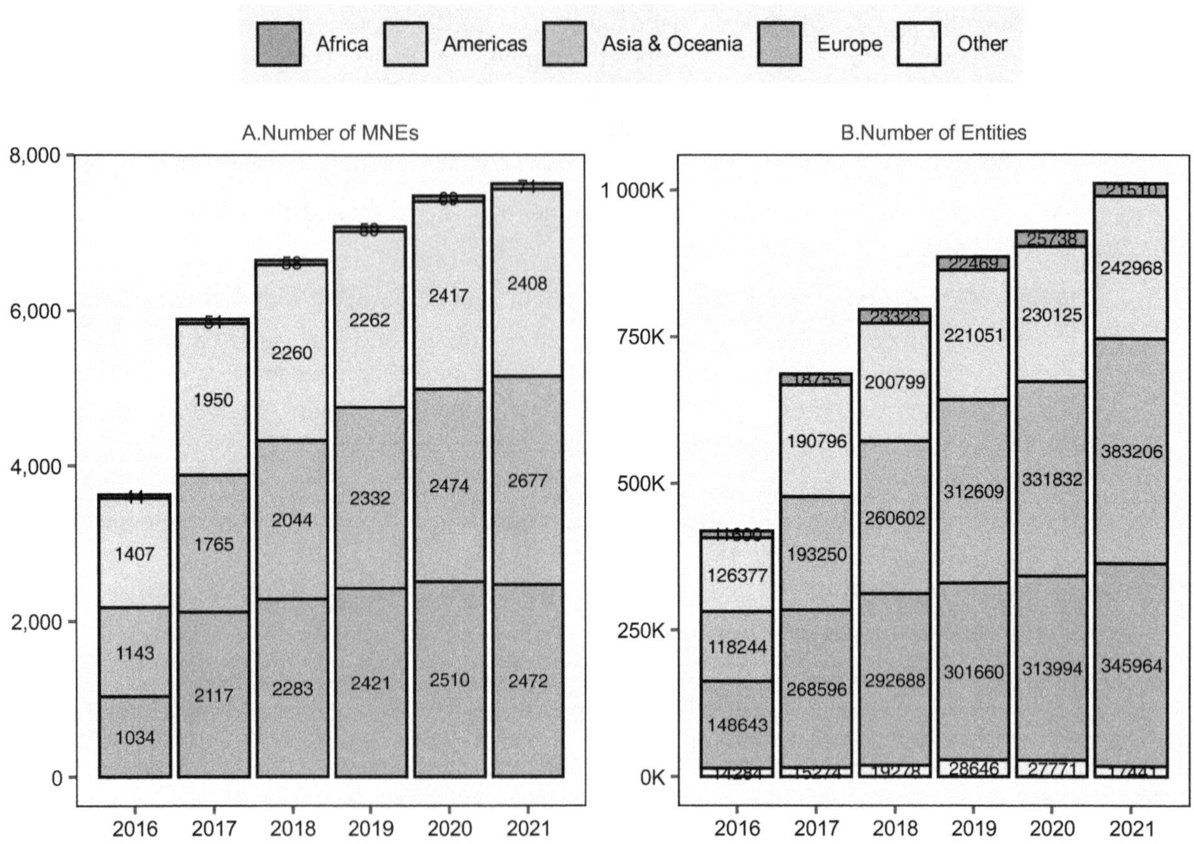

Note: K = One thousand
Source: Anonymised and aggregated CbCR statistics.

StatLink https://stat.link/3jql1t

Table 7.2. Sample composition and average values for key financial variables

	Reporting Jurisdiction	Level of data disaggregation	Number of CbCRs	Unrelated party revenues	Tangible assets (other than cash)	Income tax accrued	Number of employees
1	Andorra		Zero				
2	Argentina	18 individual jurisdictions	33	1 850	15 323	39	6 274
3	Australia	83 individual jurisdictions	148	4 802	4 266	219	10 983
4	Austria	Continents	96	4 626	2 754	69	12 711
5	Azerbaijan	34 individual jurisdictions	5	10 382	8 475	185	16 569
6	Bahrain	32 individual jurisdictions	5	1 154	986	45	5 279
7	Belgium	28 individual jurisdictions	73	4 480	3 193	91	12 548
8	Bermuda	93 individual jurisdictions	69	5 468	4 858	110	12 698
9	Brazil	34 individual jurisdictions	90	10 878	7 311	226	24 173
10	Bulgaria	4 individual jurisdictions	3	3 501	4 583	51	6 309
11	Canada	9 individual jurisdictions	220	7 509	6 803	73	17 529
12	Cayman Islands	131 individual jurisdictions	152	9 040	8 644	197	26 252
13	Chile	12 individual jurisdictions	33	5 308	6 203	194	20 554
14	China	131 individual jurisdictions	760	15 994	13 111	317	52 517
15	Czechia	All foreign jurisdictions combined					
16	Denmark	103 individual jurisdictions	78	6 067	2 812	87	16 596
17	Finland	All foreign jurisdictions combined	49	9 440	2 324	96	11 738
18	France	91 individual jurisdictions	241	11 378	5 952	303	37 110
19	Germany	161 individual jurisdictions	427	9 667	6 001	156	23 853
20	Greece	68 individual jurisdictions	14	4 206	3 052	35	11 619
21	Hong Kong (China)	141 individual jurisdictions	234	6 227	8 860	158	19 743
22	Hungary	All foreign jurisdictions combined	8	7 264	2 444	68	16 791
23	India	94 individual jurisdictions	123	9 170	15 723	231	70 922
24	Indonesia	82 individual jurisdictions	46	5 319	6 857	152	61 971
25	Ireland	All foreign jurisdictions combined	61	7 009	3 556	148	31 394
26	Italy	98 individual jurisdictions	147	6 539	3 217	107	13 277
27	Japan	136 individual jurisdictions	885	7 689	3 990	147	19 388
28	Korea	All foreign jurisdictions combined	267	8 446	7 139	202	15 458
29	Latvia	10 individual jurisdictions	3	1 360	1 530	8	2 131
30	Lithuania	7 individual jurisdictions	7	1 476	876	11	6 732
31	Luxembourg	99 individual jurisdictions	155	5 909	2 720	57	36 480
32	Malaysia	30 individual jurisdictions	59	4 126	6 495	160	17 952
33	Mauritius	Continents	8	11 314	3 770	187	7 649
34	Mexico	90 individual jurisdictions	74	6 326	4 286	228	36 379
35	Monaco		Zero				
36	Morocco	All foreign jurisdictions combined	2	5 849	7 027	266	19 153
37	Netherlands	5 individual jurisdictions	171	7 412	3 168	119	18 066
38	New Zealand	All foreign jurisdictions combined	23	3 145	2 576	34	6 362
39	Norway	60 individual jurisdictions	71	4 683	3 622	407	6 342
40	Panama	18 individual jurisdictions	5	1 076	2 809	12	12 014
41	Peru	13 individual jurisdictions	11	6 312	1 635	62	13 090
42	Portugal	46 individual jurisdictions	24	4 835	2 235	45	13 614
43	Romania	146 individual jurisdictions	4	26 577	13 717	288	66 386
44	San Marino		Zero				
45	Saudi Arabia	111 individual jurisdictions	47	21 784	34 480	4 093	17 234
46	Seychelles		Zero				
47	Singapore	28 individual jurisdictions	69	8 727	5 982	126	13 062
48	Slovenia	5 individual jurisdictions	6	3 200	934	20	5 546

	Reporting Jurisdiction	Level of data disaggregation	Number of CbCRs	Unrelated party revenues	Tangible assets (other than cash)	Income tax accrued	Number of employees
49	South Africa	33 individual jurisdictions	61	4 472	2 811	113	2 5347
50	Spain	104 individual jurisdictions	134	6 302	4 125	129	19 683
51	Sweden	Continents	117	4 502	2 243	134	14 206
52	Switzerland	135 individual jurisdictions	145	9 704	5 165	165	19 621
53	Türkiye	28 individual jurisdictions	48	6 976	2 946	106	21 044
54	Turks & Caicos Islands		Zero				
55	United Arab Emirates	148 individual jurisdictions	59	5 483	7 599	47	18 726
56	United Kingdom	Continents	390	7 653	5 863	202	17 155
57	United States	135 individual jurisdictions	1791	10 288	5 344	240	22 007
58	Surrogate Parent Filings	158 individual jurisdictions	279	11 563	8 705	198	28 453

Note: Currency values (all values except the number of CbCRs and number of employees) are reported in millions of USD. Level of data disaggregation provided depends on data confidentiality standards applicable in each reporting jurisdiction. Average values have not been calculated for Czechia as the number of CbCRs has not been supplied for confidentiality reasons.
Source: 2021 Anonymised and Aggregated CbCR statistics.

Foreign and domestic MNEs account for significant shares of CIT revenues in several jurisdictions. For a selection of countries, Figure 7.2 reports total tax accrued based on CbCR statistics, as a fraction of the total national CIT revenues, taken from the OECD's Global Revenue Statistics Database. The figure allows an examination of the relative importance of foreign and domestic MNE contributions as covered in the 2021 data.[4]

Figure 7.3 shows the variation of MNEs contribution to total CIT revenues as compared to 2020. Nineteen jurisdictions saw a net increase in the contribution of MNEs to their total CIT revenues. The percentage contribution by Chilean, Korean and Norwegian MNEs increased by over 20 percentage points (p.p.) in 2021. On the other hand, four jurisdictions saw a net decrease of more than 10 p.p. between 2020 and 2021.

MNEs operate both within their domestic jurisdiction where the UPE is located and in foreign jurisdictions where their foreign entities are located. Figure 7.4 provides detailed information about the distribution of MNE activities between domestic and foreign jurisdictions where activities operated abroad are disaggregated into regional groupings. The upward trend across most panels is in line with the increasing coverage in MNEs as depicted in Figure 7.1, however, the large decrease in total profits in 2020 can be seen as a symptom of the COVID-19 pandemic.

Panels A-D shows the location of selected financial activities, ranging from unrelated party revenues (UPR) in panel A to assets in panel D. The distribution of panel A shows that 20 out of 31 and 43 out of 69 USD trillions in UPR were located domestically in 2016 and 2021, respectively. This entails that in the years for which data is available, the majority of the activity in question takes place domestically. This trend is identical in panels B-D as well as in panel E which depicts the distribution of employees. Panel F, which captures the distribution of entities, is an exception in this respect. The figure shows that the share of domestic entities was around one third across the years 2016 to 2021.

Figure 7.2. MNEs' contribution to total CIT Revenues, 2021

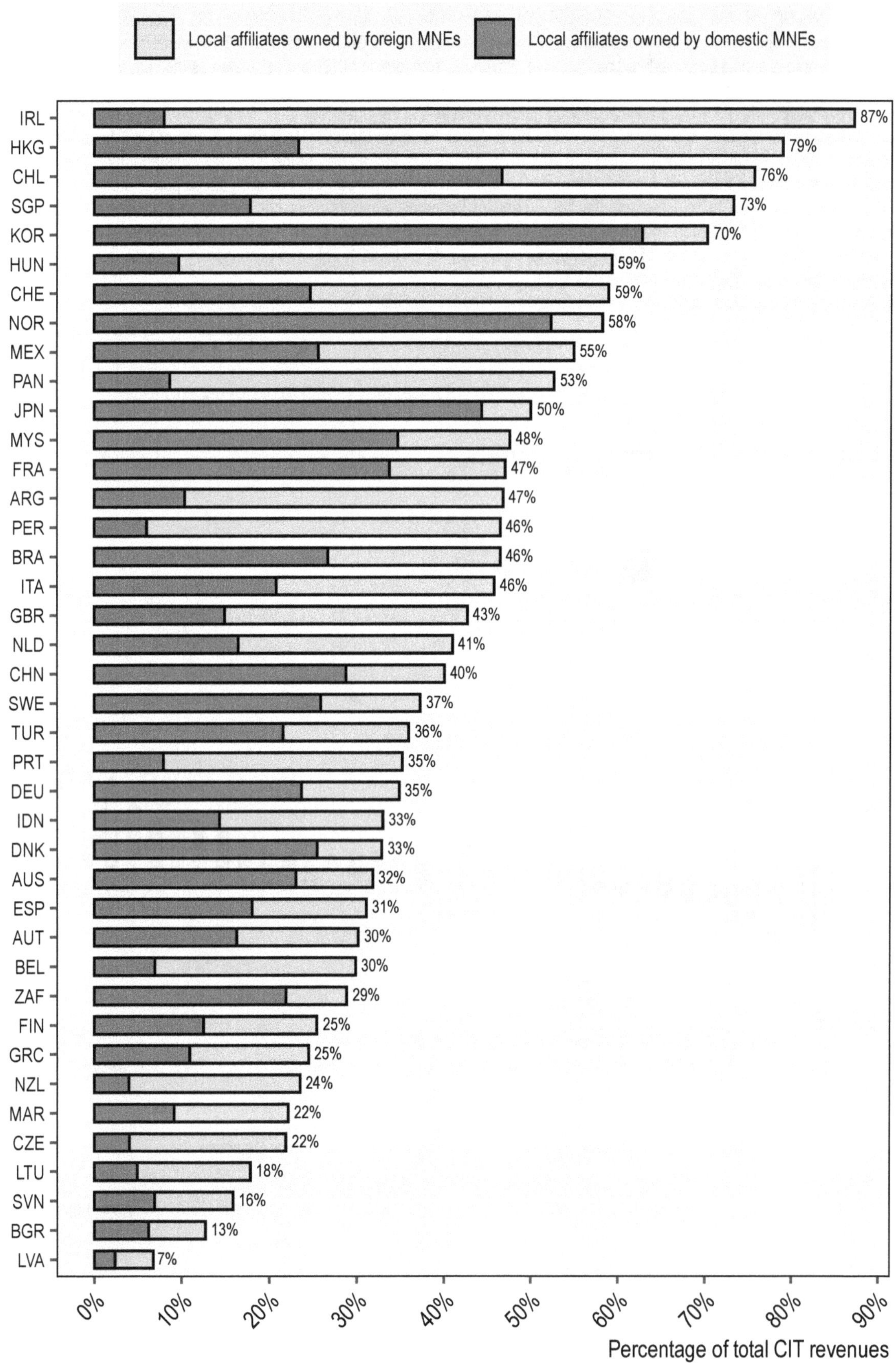

Note: The percentages above are calculated by dividing the amount of total tax accrued reported in CbCR statistics by total CIT revenues as reported in the OECD's Global Revenue Statistics Database. The figure shows total revenues of both domestic and foreign MNEs as a percentage of total CIT revenues, with jurisdictions ranked according to the total contribution of MNEs to CIT revenues. As there might be some timing differences in recording tax payments between tax accrued reported in CbCR data and CIT revenues reported in Global Revenue Statistics, percentages should be considered as indicative. Revenues from foreign MNEs are calculated as the sum of tax accrued reported in the jurisdiction by MNEs headquartered in other jurisdictions. Foreign MNEs' tax revenues should be considered as a lower bound as they can be reported exclusively where the geographical disaggregation is available at the jurisdiction level. Data for missing jurisdictions are not included because these jurisdictions are not covered in the 2021 OECD Global Revenue Statistics data. The US ratio of MNE tax revenues to total tax revenues is not presented in this chart due to a one-time transition tax imposed as part of the 2017 Tax Cuts and Jobs Act, which created a mismatch between the numerator and denominator of this ratio. MNEs generally report this transition tax as part of income taxes accrued and income taxes paid on the CbCR. However, the US Bureau of Economic Analysis does not classify this transition tax as CIT revenue (https://www.bea.gov/help/faq/1293). Therefore, the ratio of income tax accrued in CbCR data to US CIT revenues would be significantly upward biased and not indicative of the amount of CIT revenue contributed by MNEs in 2021. This mismatch is likely to persist for a number of years as taxpayers can elect to pay the tax over several years.
Source: 2021 Anonymised and Aggregated CbCR statistics and the OECD Global Revenue Statistics Database.

StatLink https://stat.link/beav2d

Figure 7.3. 2021 MNEs' contribution to total CIT Revenues compared to 2020

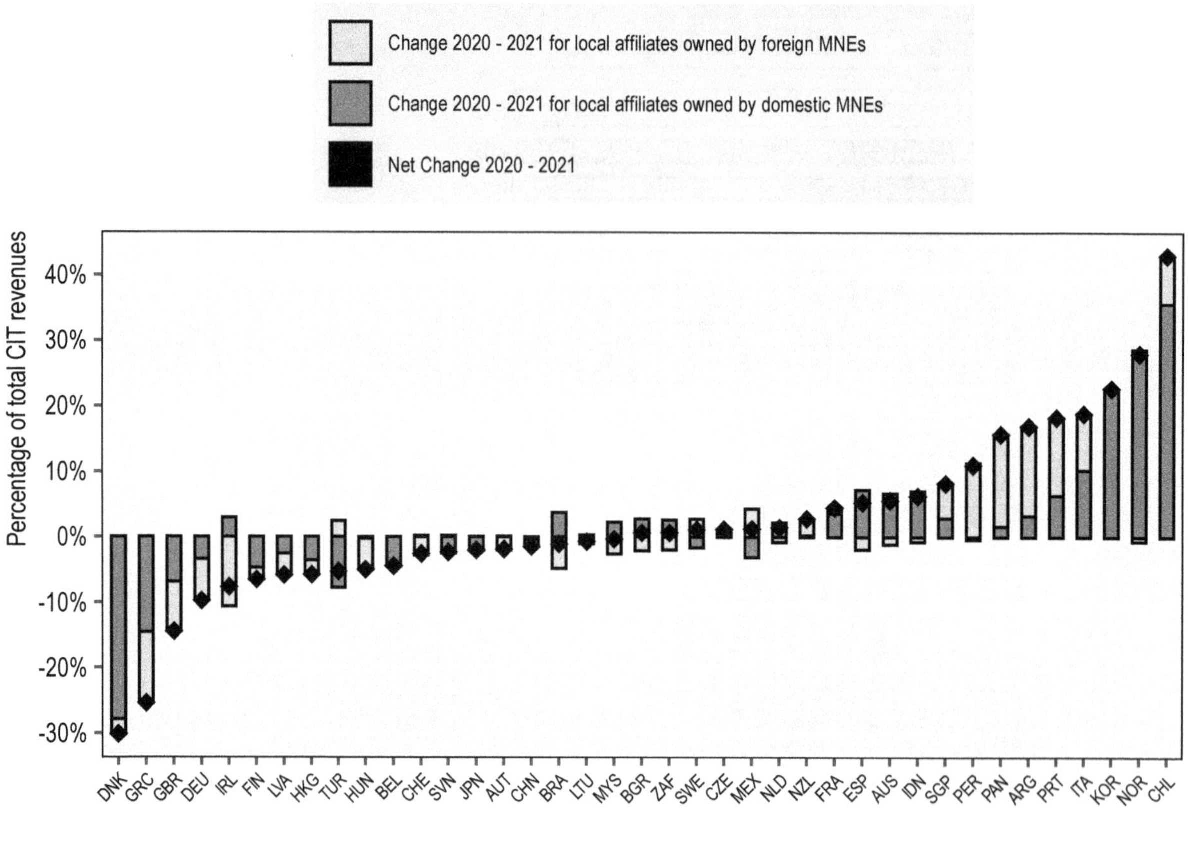

Source: Anonymised and Aggregated CbCR statistics and the OECD Global Revenue Statistics Database.

StatLink https://stat.link/gl9jiw

Figure 7.4. Domestic and foreign activities

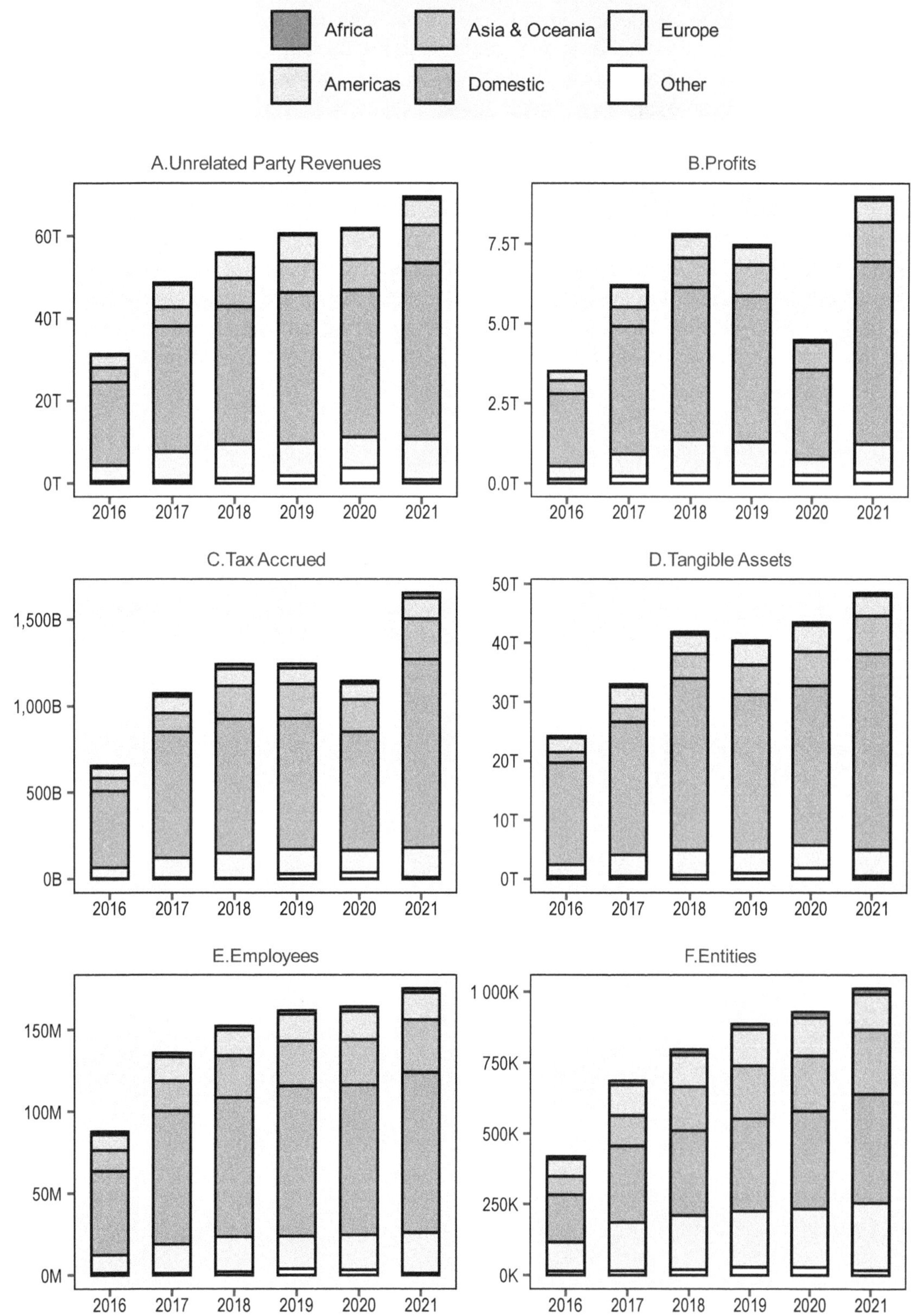

Note: T = trillions, B = billions, M = millions, K = thousands

Source: Anonymised and Aggregated CbCR statistics. These data are based on Table 1A of the CbCR statistics.

StatLink https://stat.link/nijfa9

General observations from CbCR tables

The presence and prevalence of different types of business activities may vary across regions for different reasons, including among others, the level of development, the demographic structure, trade patterns, or macroeconomic conditions. The existence of BEPS practices may also alter such prevalence in a given region. Figure 7.5 provides an overview of the business activities disaggregated into five regional groups for the most recent year for which data is available (2021).

Sales, marketing and distribution accounts for around one fifth of total business activity in four of the five regional groupings (all except "Other"). In regions with a relatively high share of low- and middle-income countries such as Africa and Asia and Oceania, manufacturing or production and provision of services are also common business activities, accounting for around 10-20% of the total number of activities in each region. Holding shares or other equity instruments are among the most popular business activities in the Other regional grouping which includes Stateless entities and those that were not disaggregated. This may be indicative of tax planning structures but could also be the result of genuine commercial activity.

Figure 7.5. Business activities by region

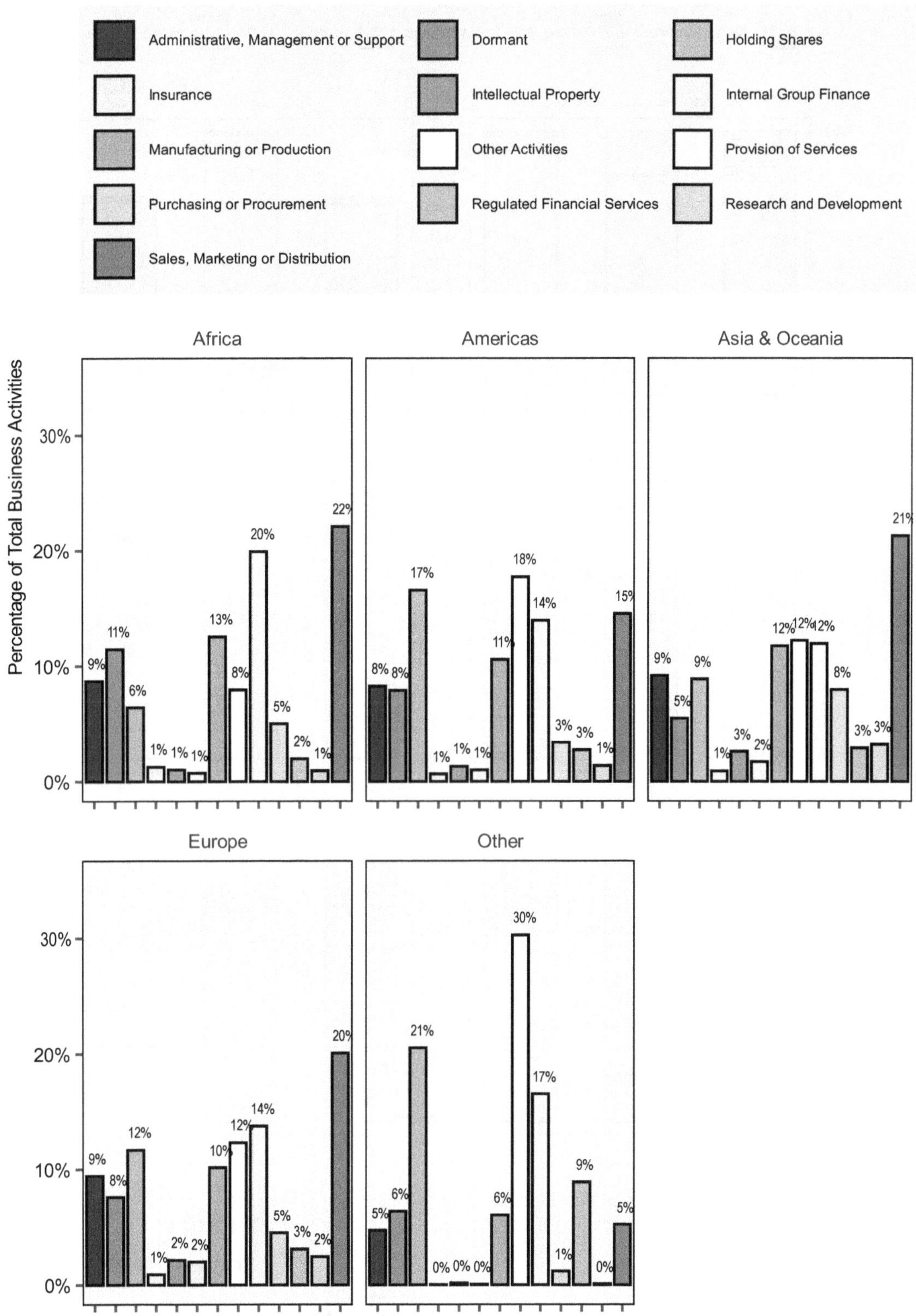

Source: 2021 Anonymised and Aggregated CbCR statistics. These data are based on the business activities data in Table 1A of the CbCR data.

StatLink https://stat.link/fm2x4o

Figure 7.6. Data disaggregated by the ETR of MNE Group

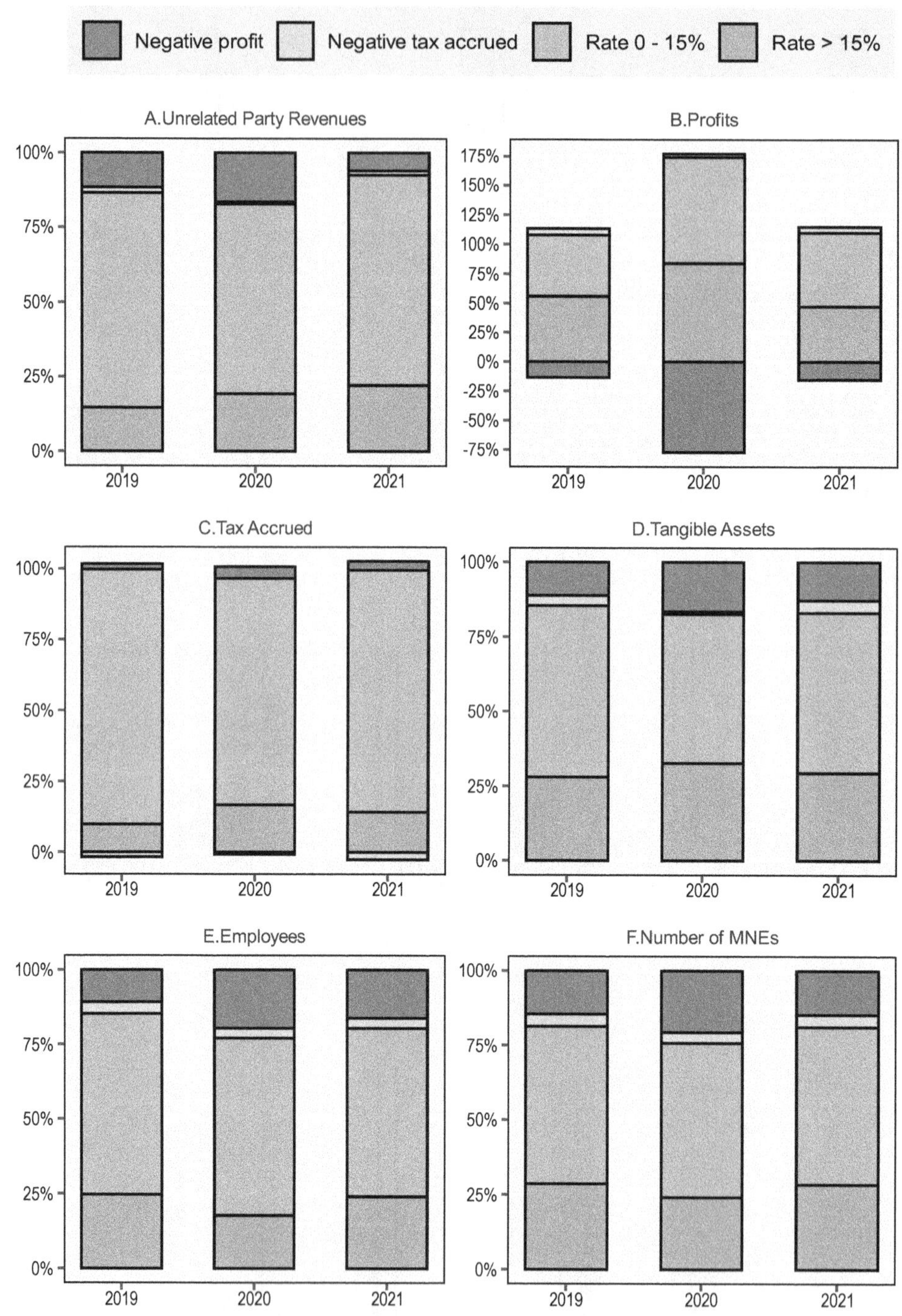

Note: Negative tax accrued refers to all MNE groups reporting positive profits with negative tax accrued.
Source: Anonymised and Aggregated CbCR statistics. These data are based on Table 4 of the CbCR statistics.

StatLink https://stat.link/fe5kj8

Figure 7.6 shows the share of different activities operated by MNEs disaggregated into four groups including MNEs for which the total profit was negative, the total profit was positive with negative total tax accrued, located in a jurisdiction with an ETR between 0 and 15%, and located in a jurisdiction with an ETR equal to or above 15%. The six available panels capture different statistics, including the number of MNEs (panel F), the number of employees (panel E), and selected financial variables (panels A-D).

The information shown in Figure 7.7 is the same as the one presented in Figure 7.6 except that the disaggregation into four groups is based on subgroup characteristics. In addition, panel F now represents the number of subgroups instead of the number of MNEs (as depicted in panel A above).

Figure 7.7 shows the share of different activities operated by MNE sub-groups disaggregated into four groups including MNEs for which the total profit was negative, the total profit was positive with negative total tax accrued, located in a jurisdiction where the ETR of the sub-group was between 0 and 15%, and located in a jurisdiction where the ETR of the sub-group was equal to or above 15%. The six available panels capture different statistics, including the number of subgroups (panel F), the number of employees (panel E), and selected financial variables (panels A-D).

The size of MNE groups varies across the sample and includes a small number of relatively large MNE groups. Figure 7.8 shows the distribution points of unrelated party revenues of MNE groups headquartered in each reporting jurisdiction. A common feature across all jurisdictions is that the mean MNE size in terms of unrelated party revenues is considerably larger than the median size, indicating that the underlying sample includes a small number of relatively large MNE groups.

Key insights on BEPS from CbCR data

This release of anonymised and aggregated CbCR data (FY 2021) provides some insights on BEPS.

Due to the limitations of the CbCR data, considerable caution needs to be exercised when attempting to draw conclusions about BEPS from the data. This is especially the case given that this is only the sixth year for which anonymised and aggregated data have been provided. Six years of data can give only limited insights on changes and potential trends in BEPS behaviour. In addition, the comparability between the 2016 sample and the samples for 2017 to 2021 is limited due to the move from voluntary to mandatory filing in some countries and differences in fiscal year coverage (see Box 7.2). Taking these caveats into account, the 2024 release of CbCR statistics suggests some insights on BEPS:

There is evidence of misalignment between the location where profits are reported and the location where economic activities occur. The data show continuing differences in the distribution across jurisdiction groups of employees, tangible assets, and profits.[5] Figure 7.9 presents the distribution of MNEs' foreign activities across jurisdiction groups.[6] For example, high and middle income jurisdictions account for a higher share of total employees (respectively 37% and 44%) and total tangible assets (respectively 38% and 32%) than of profits (respectively 32% and 24%). On the other hand, in investment hubs, on average, MNEs report a relatively high share of profits (18%) compared to their share of employees (4%) and tangible assets (12%). High income jurisdictions, middle income jurisdictions, and investment hubs account for 36%, 32%, and 11% of tax accrued, respectively.[7]

Revenues and profits per employee tend to be higher in investment hubs. Figure 7.10 and Figure 7.11 shows that the ratio of total revenues and profits to the number of employees is higher in investment hubs. In investment hubs, median revenues per employee are USD 1 638 000 while in high-, middle- and low-income jurisdictions median revenues per employee are USD 504 000, USD 210 000 and USD 226 000 respectively. While this may reflect differences in capital intensity or in worker productivity, it is likely also at least partially an indicator of BEPS.

There is some evidence that the extent of misalignment may be decreasing in recent years. Revenue per employee in investment hubs has fallen from USD 1 885 000 in 2017 to USD to USD 1 638 000 in 2021. By contrast the ratio of profits to employees in other jurisdictions has increased to USD 24 000 (from USD 20 000) for high income jurisdictions and to USD 17 000 (from USD 4 000) for low-income jurisdictions. Investment hubs share of total taxes paid has remained steady at around 11% across all years, while investment hubs share of total MNE profits has fallen from 28.2% in 2017 to 18.4% in 2021. A variety of factors can be driving these figures, notably given the significant economic turbulence in recent years. However, that these data may also be an indicator of reduced BEPS behaviour.

Figure 7.7. Data disaggregated by the ETR of MNE sub-group

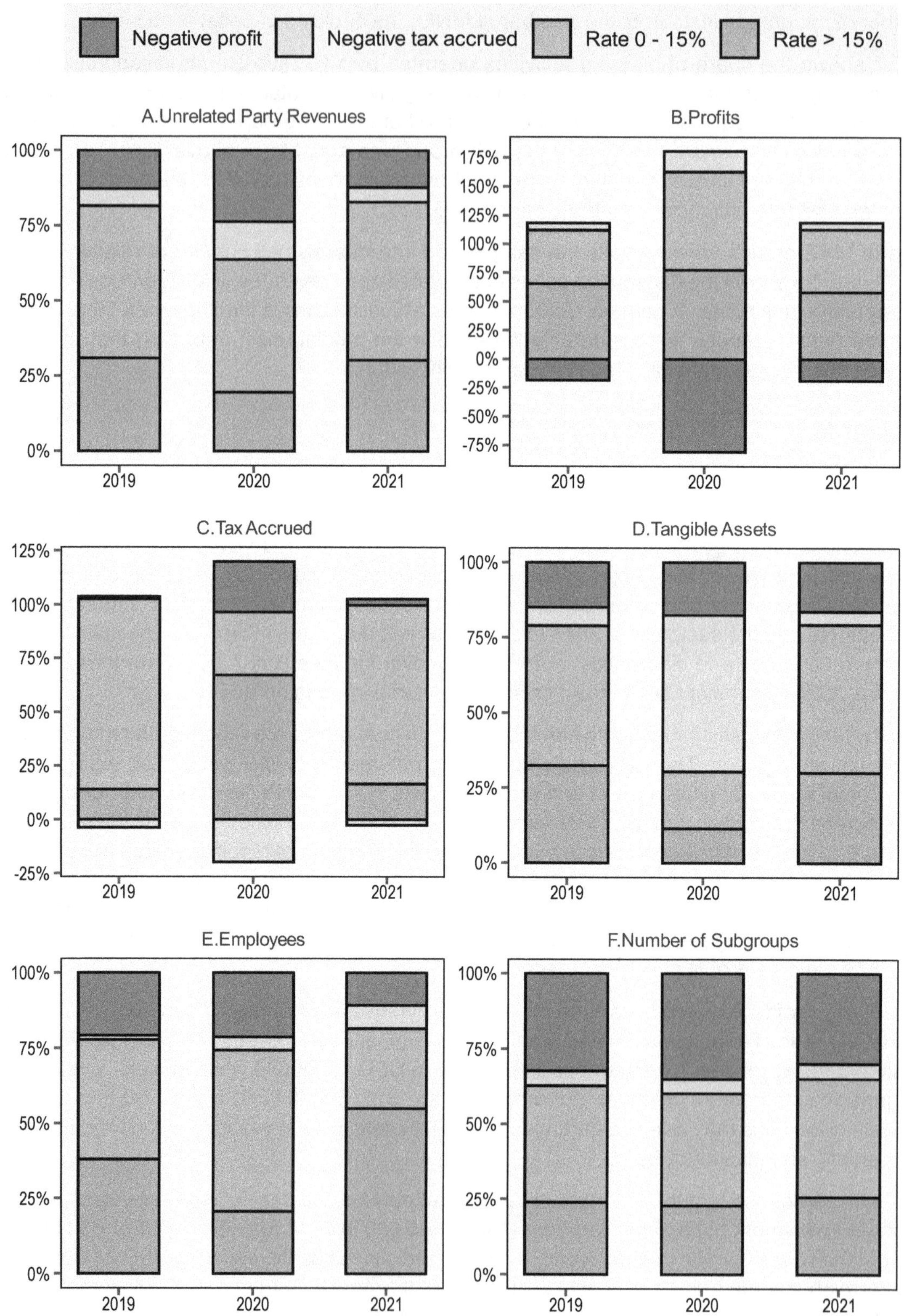

Note: Negative tax accrued refers to all MNE sub-groups reporting positive profits with negative tax accrued.
Source: Anonymised and Aggregated CbCR statistics. These data are based on Table 5 of the CbCR statistics.

StatLink https://stat.link/3zecu5

Figure 7.8. Distribution of MNE unrelated party revenues by ultimate parent jurisdiction

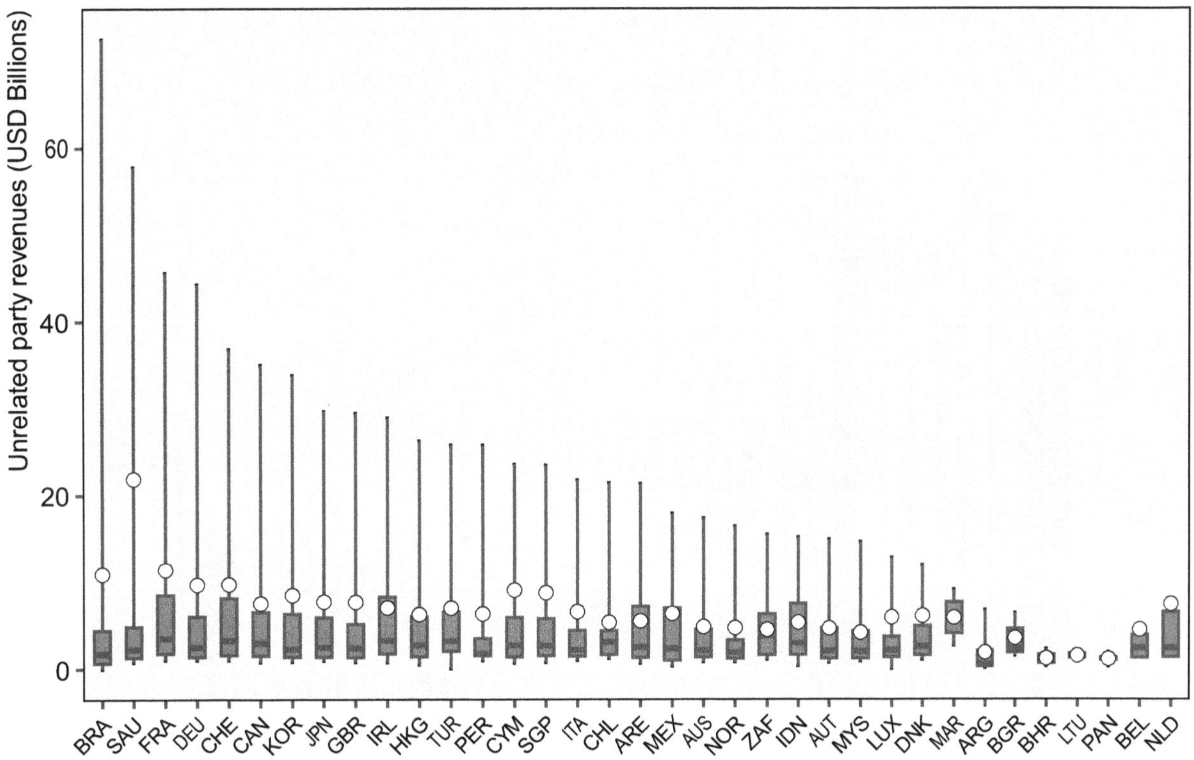

Note: The white dot represents the average value (obtained by dividing totals by the number of CbCRs), the blue boxes are delimited by the 25th and 75th percentiles, thus representing 50% of the sample within each jurisdiction. The horizontal black bar shows the median (50th percentile). The two whiskers indicate the 5th and 95th percentiles. Jurisdictions are ranked with respect to the 95th percentile where available. Country coverage reflects data availability in Table 6 of the CbCR data.
Source: 2021 Anonymised and Aggregated CbCR statistics.

StatLink https://stat.link/obsazv

On average, the share of related party revenues in total revenues is higher for MNEs in certain jurisdictions. Figure 7.12 plots the distribution of related party revenues as a share of total revenues, by jurisdiction group. On average, the share of related party revenues in total revenues is higher in investment hubs than in high-, middle- and low-income jurisdictions. In investment hubs, related party revenues account for over 30% of total revenues, whereas the median share of related party revenues in high-, and middle-income jurisdictions is 18% and 14% respectively. The median share of related party revenues in low-income jurisdictions is much lower at just 7%. While high levels of related party revenues may be commercially motivated, they are also a high-level risk assessment factor and could be evidence of tax planning. Investment hubs share of related party revenues has declined in recent years, from 37% in 2017 to 33% in 2021.

The composition of business activity differs across jurisdiction groups. Figure 7.13 shows the share of main business activities in each jurisdiction group. In high-, middle- and low-income jurisdictions, sales, manufacturing, and services are the most prevalent activities, while in investment hubs the predominant activity is "holding shares" which also includes other equity instruments. A concentration of holding companies is a risk assessment factor and could be indicative of certain tax planning structures. However, as with related party revenues, this observation may also relate to genuine commercial arrangements.

Figure 7.9. Jurisdiction groups' shares of foreign MNEs' activities

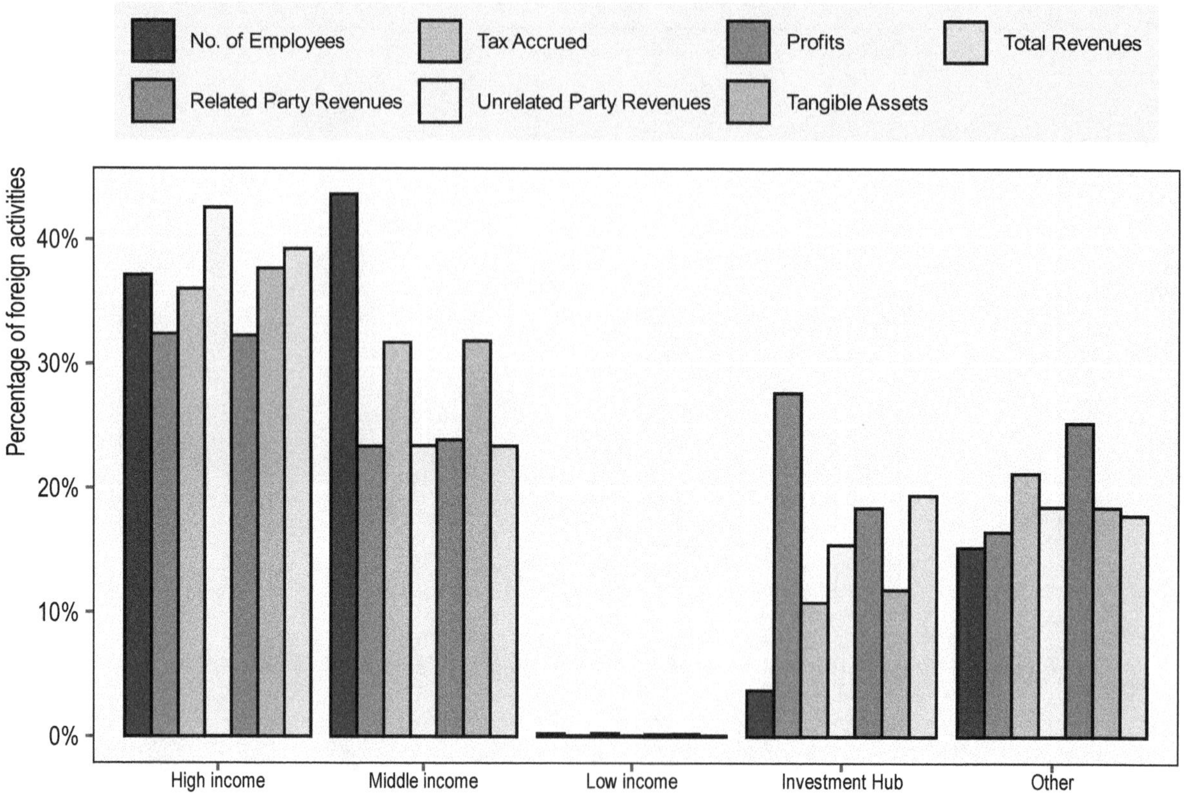

Note: The profit variable could include intracompany dividends in several instances and therefore be upward biased. The bars represent jurisdiction groups' shares of different variables (e.g., profit in group x/total profits booked in foreign jurisdictions) across all jurisdictions included in the CbCR sample. The percentages are calculated using Table 1A Panel A (all subgroups). "Other" reflects aggregate geographic groupings and Stateless entities.
Source: 2021 Anonymised and Aggregated CbCR statistics.

StatLink https://stat.link/bt1elp

Figure 7.10. Median profits per employee: distribution within jurisdiction groups

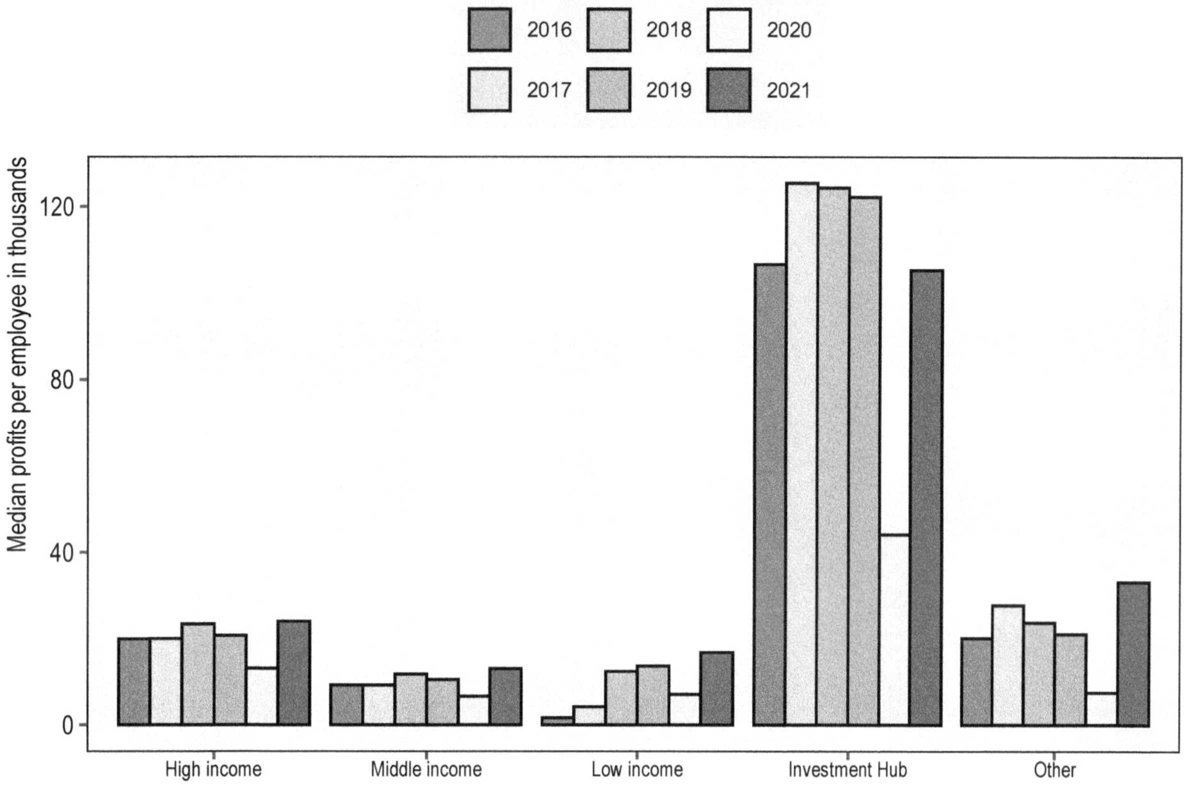

Note: "Other" reflects aggregate geographic groupings and Stateless entities.
Source: 2021 Anonymised and Aggregated CbCR statistics.

StatLink https://stat.link/2hcipq

Figure 7.11. Median total revenues per employee: Distribution within jurisdiction groups

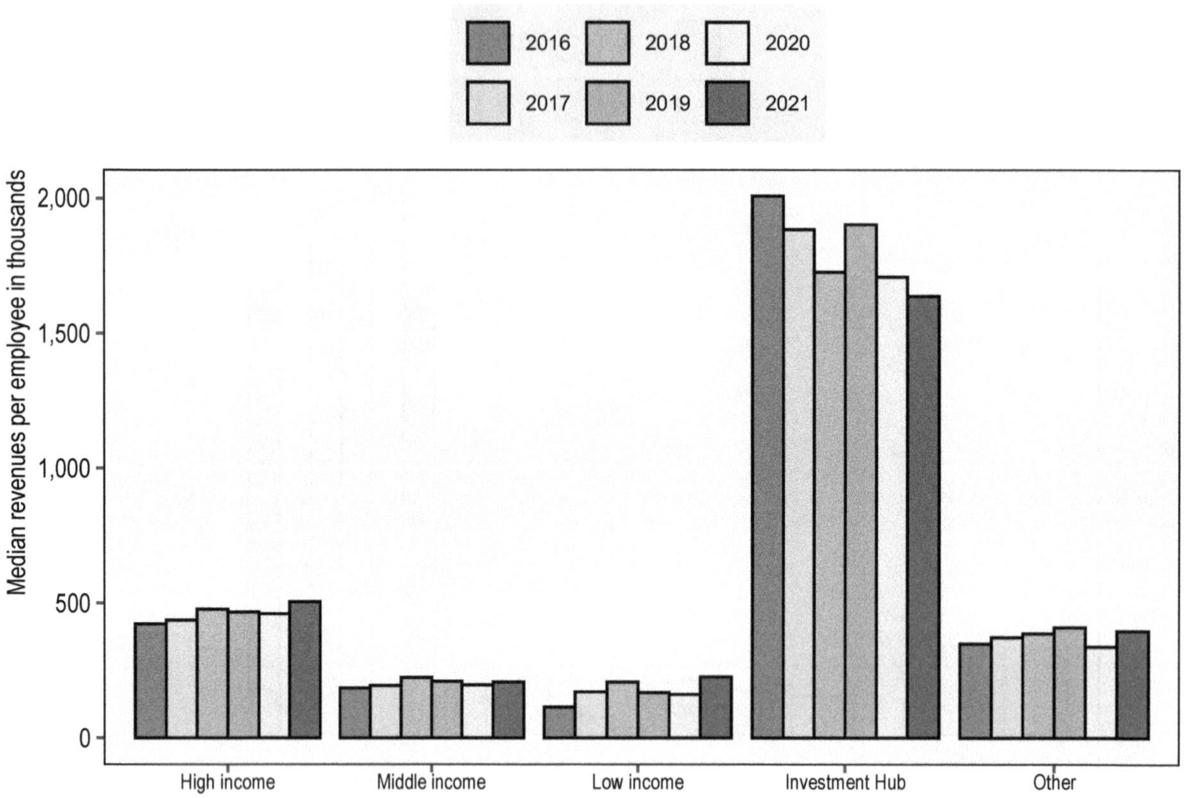

Note: "Other" reflects aggregate geographic groupings and Stateless entities.
Source: 2021 Anonymised and Aggregated CbCR statistics.

StatLink https://stat.link/cuojzf

Figure 7.12. Median related party revenues shares: Distribution within jurisdiction groups

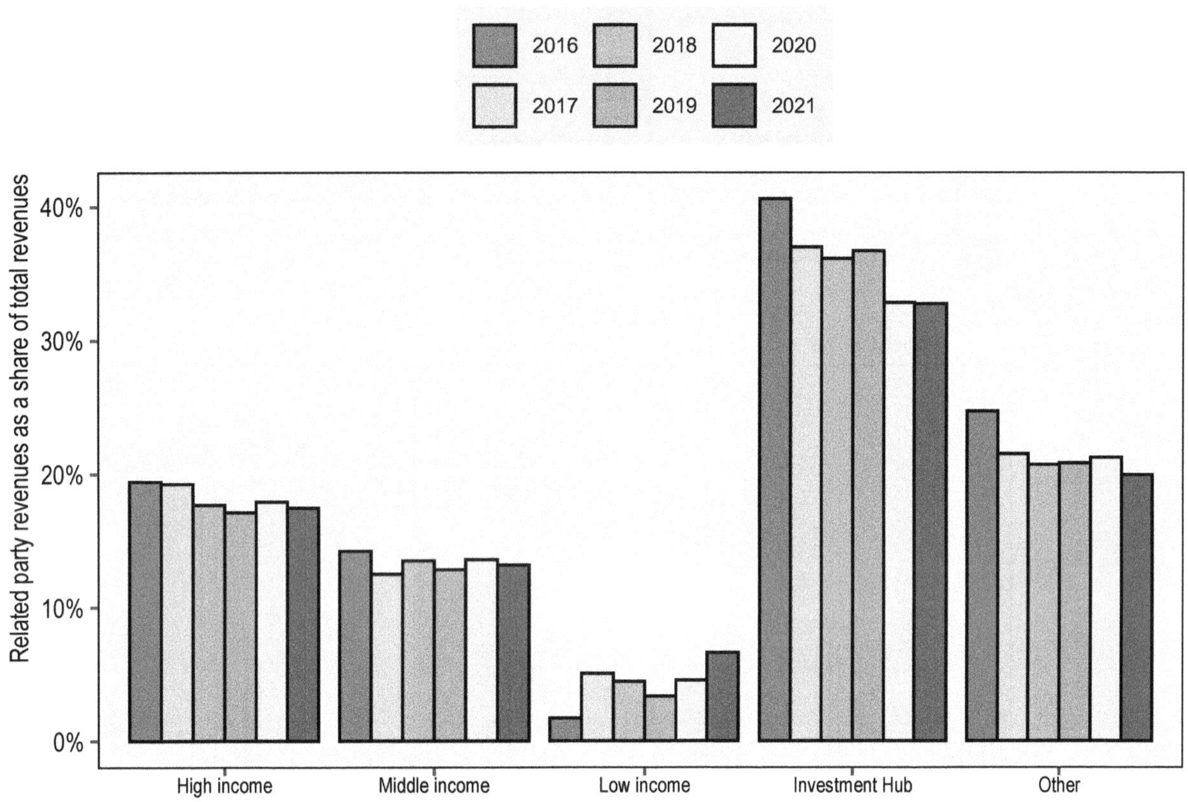

Note: The chart displays the distribution of related party revenues as a share of total revenues within each jurisdiction group. "Other" reflects aggregate geographic groupings and Stateless entities.
Source: 2021 Anonymised and Aggregated CbCR statistics.

StatLink https://stat.link/5gj76c

Figure 7.13. Business activities performed across jurisdiction groups

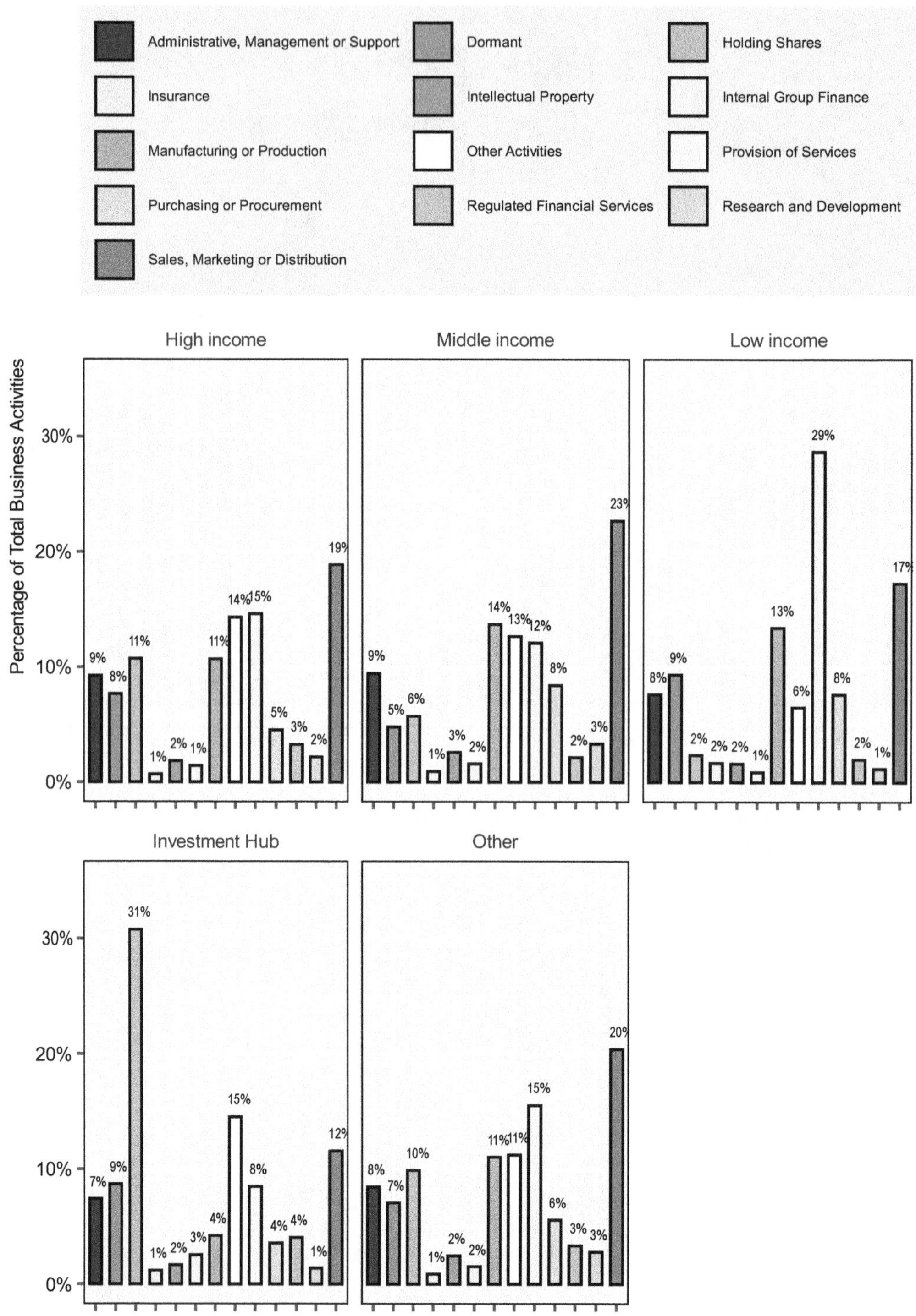

Note: The ratios are calculated by dividing the number of the activities performed in a jurisdiction group by the total number of all activities performed in this jurisdiction group where data is available. For example, 19% of all activities performed in high income jurisdictions are in the "sales" category. Entities could be attributed to one or more of the following activities: research and development; holding or managing IP; purchasing or procurement; manufacturing or production (manufacturing); sales, marketing or distribution (sales); administrative, management or support services; provision of services to unrelated parties (services); internal group finance; regulated financial services; insurance; holding shares or other equity instruments (holding shares); dormant; other activities. For the United States, other activities also include holding or managing IP; insurance; internal group finance; and research and development.
Source: 2021 Anonymised and Aggregated CbCR statistics

StatLink https://stat.link/qzt6un

References

OECD (2015), *Measuring and Monitoring BEPS, Action 11 - 2015 Final Report*, OECD/G20 Base Erosion and Profit Shifting Project, OECD Publishing, Paris, https://doi.org/10.1787/9789264241343-en. [1]

Notes

[1] In the case of the United States, CbCR data are less granular than Inland Revenue Service (IRS) Form 5471, 8865, and 8858 data.

[2] With the exception of stateless income, which could relate to either domestic or foreign activities.

[3] The total number of MNEs covered in the 2021 CbCR statistics is 8030. This includes all headquarter MNEs, MNEs that provide foreign information only and MNEs that have chosen surrogate filing.

[4] Foreign MNEs' contributions might be understated for two main reasons: first, some jurisdictions provided limited geographical disaggregation; second, the contributions of MNEs with parents headquartered in jurisdictions that did not provide data are missing.

[5] As indicated in Box 7.2, and described in greater detail at http://www.oecd.org/tax/tax-policy/anonymised-and-aggregated-cbcr-statistics-disclaimer.pdf, profits may be overestimated due to the inclusion of intra-company dividends. To evaluate the potential magnitude of included dividends country specific analyses are available at: Netherlands: https://oe.cd/3Kp; Ireland: https://oe.cd/3Kn; Italy: https://oe.cd/3Ko; Sweden: https://oe.cd/3Kq; United Kingdom: https://oe.cd/3Kr.

[6] Jurisdiction groups (high, middle and low income) are based on the World Bank classification resulting in 61 high income jurisdictions, 104 middle income jurisdictions, and 29 low-income jurisdictions. Investment hubs are defined as jurisdictions with a total inward Foreign Direct Investment (FDI) position above 150% of gross domestic product (GDP).

[7] Tax accrued depends on both effective tax rates and taxable profits in a jurisdiction.

www.ingramcontent.com/pod-product-compliance
Lightning Source LLC
Chambersburg PA
CBHW061223240926
51846CB00006B/1334
* 9 7 8 9 2 6 4 5 0 0 8 1 5 *